Teaching Advanced Language Skills through Global Debate

Mastering Languages through Global Debate Textbooks

Mastering English Through Global Debate
Ekaterina Talalakina, Tony Brown, Jennifer Bown,
and William Eggington

Mastering Russian Through Global Debate
Tony Brown, Tatiana Balykhina, Ekaterina Talalakina, Jennifer Bown,
and Viktoria Kurilenko

Mastering Chinese Through Global Debate
Dana Bourgerie, Rachel Yu Liu, and Lin Qi,
foreword by Cornelius Kubler

Teaching Advanced Language Skills through Global Debate

Theory and Practice

Tony Brown and Jennifer Bown

GEORGETOWN UNIVERSITY PRESS

The publisher is not responsible for third-party websites or their content. URL links were active at time of publication.

Library of Congress Cataloging-in-Publication Data

Names: Brown, Tony (Newel Anthony), author. | Bown, Jennifer, author.
Title: Teaching advanced language skills through global debate : theory and practice / Tony Brown and Jennifer Bown.
Description: Washington, DC : Georgetown University Press, 2016. | Includes bibliographical references.
Identifiers: LCCN 2016030257 (print) | LCCN 2016040668 (ebook) | ISBN 9781626164307 (pb : alk. paper) | ISBN 9781626161443 (eb) | ISBN 9781626161443 (e-book)
Subjects: LCSH: Language and languages—Ability testing. | Language and languages—Study and teaching. | Second language acquisition. | Debates and debating.
Classification: LCC P53.4 .B767 2016 (print) | LCC P53.4 (ebook) | DDC 418.0071—dc23
LC record available at https://lccn.loc.gov/2016030257

♾ This book is printed on acid-free paper meeting the requirements of the American National Standard for Permanence in Paper for Printed Library Materials.

18 17   9 8 7 6 5 4 3 2   First printing

Printed in the United States of America

This publication was originally released as born-digital content. The links in the digital edition are not available in this print edition. Please refer to the ebook to access the linking features.

Contents

Introduction

Rationale

For centuries, debate has played a prominent role in universities through-out Western Europe and the United States. In addition to educating students about significant social and political issues, debate fosters critical thinking and analytical skills as well as respect for opposing opinions and an increased capacity to relate to others. In a debate, every claim is subject to questioning, thus creating an environment rich in rhetorical strategies and complex linguistic constructions.

Because of its public nature, debate also demands a sophisticated level of public speaking ability that extends beyond mere narration and descrip-tion to persuasion and support of a hypothesis or claim. From the stand-point of language proficiency, the very criteria that constitute a well-educated native speaker likewise constitute an articulate debater. For example, the American Council on the Teaching of Foreign Languages (ACTFL) notes that speakers at the Superior level can "present their opinions on a number of issues of interest to them, provide structured arguments to support these opinions, and . . . develop hypotheses to explore alternative possibilities" (ACTFL 2012, 5). Given the striking similarities between debate and Superior-level proficiency, the question arises as to whether debate can contribute to Superior-level second language (L2) proficiency.

Our efforts to answer this question began in earnest in 2007 with the creation of a course titled Global Debate, and culminated in 2014 with the publication of two foreign language textbooks in which parliamentary-style debate and exercises devoted to building debate skills serve as a means for developing Advanced- and Superior-level proficiency.[1] This volume expands on the innovative approach introduced in the aforementioned textbook series, Mastering Languages through Global Debate, and underscores the importance of well-planned university foreign language instruction as a critical step toward achieving proficiency gain.

Overview of Textbook Objective and Components

The series Mastering Languages through Global Debate is designed for students who have attained Advanced-level proficiency. Its primary objective is to foster the language and critical thinking skills necessary for conducting successful debates. In order to progress from Advanced- to Superior-level proficiency, learners must be able to discuss abstract topics, express and support opinions, hypothesize, and tailor their language to specific audiences. Debate offers a powerful forum for developing and honing this skill set. Textbooks in the series comprise six chapters, each one addressing a different debate topic: Economy versus Environment, Interventionism versus Isolationism, Wealth Redistribution versus Self-Reliance, Cultural Preservation versus Diversity, Security versus Freedom, and Education versus Field Experience.

Each chapter begins with exercises to activate the learners' background knowledge. These exercises allow students to articulate their own ideas on each of the topics and prepare them for reading the texts that comprise the heart of each chapter. These texts are not simplified in any way and thus provide a rich source of input, particularly in terms of contextualized vocabulary. Each text also presents an overview of the topics, including the major arguments on both sides of the debate, followed by comprehension checks. This approach to foreign language learning builds on Boris Shekhtman's island theory, according to which a text provides model sentences that learners can "swim" to for safety. Such sentences offer a template from which to create new sentences that contain similar lexical items and follow the same logical structure (Leaver and Shekhtman 2002). Sufficient repetition of an island leads to automatization and, particularly for Superior-level speakers, the ability to produce the island quickly and appropriately in relation to any given topic.

A major portion of each chapter is dedicated to vocabulary development. Lexical items are introduced not as single words but rather as collocations—groups of words commonly used together. The choice of vocabulary in each chapter was governed in part by frequency of use as found in linguistic corpora. The text often directs students to use online corpora to further their word knowledge so that they learn words as they are used in context, not in isolation. Open-ended discussion questions offer a starting point for learners to apply new vocabulary introduced in the articles.

Once students have become acquainted with a topic and the vocabulary necessary for discussion, they turn their attention to preparing for the debate. Learners are introduced to advanced syntactical features of the language, particularly those used to form hypotheses—a function necessary in order to perform at the Superior level. They put their new knowledge to use in a role-play by representing various stakeholders discussing the issue in a concrete way. In addition, learners listen to brief mock debates that illustrate important turns of phrases used for turn taking, arguing a point, agreeing, and disagreeing.

Written position papers followed by oral debates represent the culminating tasks for the textbook. With regard to writing, learners are introduced to the elements of persuasive writing, from writing a thesis statement to constructing paragraphs and, finally, revising the essay. In terms of speaking, learners are introduced to important rhetorical strategies used in debate, such as conjecture, questions of definition, and questions of value. Ultimately, learners put their skills to the test both in a persuasive essay and in an oral debate.

1

Overview of Proficiency Guidelines

Description of Assessment Criteria for
ACTFL Advanced and Superior Levels

The year 2012 marked thirty years since the initial development of the ACTFL provisional proficiency guidelines for speaking (as part of the ACTFL Language Proficiency Projects in 1982).[2] The introduction of the guidelines sparked a proficiency movement in foreign language instruction as instructors became more concerned about what learners could *do* with the language rather than with what they *knew* about the language. Nevertheless, in 1998 Erwin Tschirner and L. Kathy Heilenman published the results of their examination of key studies of correlation between length of postsecondary language study and oral proficiency interview (OPI) ratings. Their meta-analysis revealed a mean rating of Intermediate Mid for students who completed two years of instruction, Intermediate High after three years, and Advanced Low after four years.

However, in the years since September 11, 2001, in particular, producing speakers with Superior-level proficiency has become a national priority. Not only has the outside world demanded users of languages at these levels for purposes of national security, but learners themselves have sought higher proficiency levels in order to take advantage of growing opportunities to use language skills in ways unimaginable just a few decades ago.

Defining Our Terms: What Does a Rating of Advanced or Superior on an OPI Tell Us?

In this volume, references to Advanced or Superior, according to the ACTFL proficiency guidelines, act as orientation descriptors for discussing higher levels of language use; therefore, it is important that the reader understand (1) how an OPI is administered, (2) what a rating in the Advanced or Superior range says about a speaker, and (3) what rating criteria are used for each level.

An official ACTFL OPI is conducted by a certified ACTFL tester either over the phone or in person, is recorded, and lasts between fifteen and thirty minutes. After the interview, the tester listens to the OPI recording in order to assign a rating. The OPI is then blind second-rated by another certified tester. If the first and second ratings do not agree exactly, the OPI is sent to a master tester or trainer for arbitration before a final rating is issued.[3] The OPI itself is a "criteria referenced assessment," with the criteria being those set forth in the *ACTFL Proficiency Guidelines 2012*—Speaking. The focus of the guidelines is on the speaker's functional ability to perform certain tasks at each major level of the scale (Novice, Intermediate, Advanced, Superior). As a result of this focus on functional language use, an OPI can be used to assess the proficiency of any language user, regardless of his or her profile (a true second or foreign language learner, or a heritage or native speaker) and of how or where the language being assessed was learned or acquired. This focus on function also arguably explains the resiliency and flexibility of these guidelines since their conceptualization, which have enabled them to endure for decades in various contexts.[4]

The assessment criterion related to expected functions for a given level is referred to as Global Tasks and Functions. The "list," so to speak, of functions is limited at each major level of the scale: Novice speakers can use memorized material, such as formulaic language, and they produce memorized lists in highly familiar topic domains; Intermediate speakers can create with the language to engage in simple conversation, ask questions, and handle a simple social transaction; Advanced speakers can narrate and describe in major time frames and handle a situation with an unexpected complication; and Superior speakers can discuss abstract issues extensively, support opinions, hypothesize, and handle linguistically unfamiliar situations. Following is a more detailed discussion of the Advanced and Superior functions, but it should be noted here that these lists of functions required at each major level are limited, meaning that an official OPI simply might not elicit or document many things that a speaker at a given level can or cannot do. All speakers who receive the same major rating on an official ACTFL OPI have one thing in common: they can perform the required functions for the level assigned and, unless rated Superior, cannot sustain performance of the required tasks at the next higher level.[5]

In addition to the category of Global Tasks and Functions, there are three other major assessment criteria used to rate a speaker's language proficiency (discussed in detail in the following): Content/Context, Comprehensibility (including Accuracy), and Text Type. These other assessment criteria are logical extensions of what a speaker's language actually has to be like in order to accomplish the functions of a given level. In order to be rated at a given major level, a speaker must sustain all of the criteria for the level over the course of the interview. The discussions presented in this volume of teaching, learning, and assessing at the levels of ACTFL Advanced and Superior are predicated upon a common understanding of how these criteria are defined and assessed in an actual OPI.

What Does a Rating in the Advanced Range Mean?

Speakers rated in the ACTFL Advanced range must be able to perform the following functions: narrating and describing in major time frames and handling situations in everyday social transactions that include an unexpected complication. In terms of the assessment criterion of Content/Context, the speaker must demonstrate the ability to perform Advanced-level functions across a range of concrete topic areas that include not only the autobiographical and familiar but also more general topic domains related to work as well as topics of interest to the broader community, whether local, national, or even international news. We think of an Advanced speaker as a "reporter." The criterion Comprehensibility/Accuracy includes linguistic features such as pronunciation, intonation patterns, tones for tonal languages, and pace or "fluency" as well as structural control including grammar and syntax. These features are assessed in two primary ways in an official OPI: (1) In relation to the level of accuracy required to perform the function, are these linguistic features adequate to perform successfully the communicative task at the intended level? and (2) in relation to the kind of listener required for successful communication, does the speaker need a very sympathetic listener accustomed to dealing with nonnatives in order to be understood, or a neutral, nonsympathetic listener? In order to be rated ACTFL Advanced, the speaker must control the basic structures of the language sufficiently (not perfectly!) so as not to miscommunicate or confuse the listener when performing Advanced-level functions. At the Advanced level, a speaker should no longer need a "sympathetic listener" in order to communicate. In terms of the assessment criteria of Text Type, paragraph-type oral discourse is required for a rating in the Advanced range because that is the text type required by the functions, such as narrations and descriptions. A speaker who produces only simple sentences, for example, simply will not be able to perform Advanced-level functions; a more sophisticated text type (such as extended discourse) is not required in order to perform those same functions.

A word about the sublevel ratings: A speaker rated Advanced Low can perform the functions of Advanced while sustaining the other assessment criteria, albeit minimally. At Advanced Low, a speaker does not usually show any evidence of Superior-level criteria. A speaker rated Advanced Mid is a speaker who performs the functions of Advanced while sustaining the other assessment criteria with good quantity and quality across a range of topics. A speaker rated Advanced Mid is likely to show some evidence of performance and linguistic features associated with the Superior. An Advanced High speaker is able to perform Superior-level functions most of the time but is not able to sustain that performance across a range of functions and topic areas. A rating of Advanced High is not just a superstar when performing Advanced functions; rather, an Advanced High should be thought of as an "almost Superior."

What Does a Rating of Superior Mean?

The Global Tasks and Functions that a speaker must demonstrate to achieve a rating of ACTFL Superior include discussing an issue at the abstract level, supporting opinion, hypothesizing, and handling "linguistically unfamiliar situations" (usually indicated by the ability to circumlocute and to deal with any low-frequency or unfamiliar linguistic material). A Superior speaker is one who can "think aloud" in the target language about a range of general issues. In terms of the assessment criteria of Content/Context, this criterion expands to include most practical, social, and professional (not highly specialized) topics as well as settings where these topics might be discussed. In terms of the criterion of Comprehensibility/Accuracy, a Superior speaker is able to communicate effectively with speakers not used to dealing with learners; errors may occur, but they are sporadic (not patterned) and neither impede communication nor distract the listener from the message. In terms of the assessment criteria of Text Type, the ability to produce and control extended discourse is required for a rating of Superior because that is the text type required by the functions; less sophisticated text type simply will prove inadequate when a speaker is attempting Superior-level functions.

Description of Assessment Criteria for the Common European Framework of Reference

While ACTFL's proficiency scales are the accepted norm in the United States, most of Europe follows a set of guidelines known as the Common European Framework of Reference for Languages: Learning, Teaching, and Assessment (CEFR). The CEFR describes what a learner can do at six specific levels: A1, A2, B1, B2, C1, and C2, which correspond to three basic descriptors:

- Basic User (A1 and A2)
- Independent User (B1 and B2)
- Proficient User (C1 and C2)

While attempts to correlate the ACTFL and CEFR scales have met with mixed results, descriptors indicate that B2, C1, and C2 may well correspond to ACTFL's Advanced High, Superior, and possibly even Distinguished levels.

For each level, the CEFR describes in depth the competencies necessary for effective communication skills and the situations (people, place, time, organization, etc.) and contexts (study, work, social, tourism, etc.) in which communication takes place.

The CEFR includes a global scale that describes the general competencies of learners at each of the six levels and includes descriptors of "qualities of spoken language" as well as a set of specific descriptors for a variety of language tasks. Whereas ACTFL stops with global descriptions of listening, speaking, reading, and writing proficiency, the CEFR scale includes separate descriptors for specific tasks. For example, with regard to speaking, the CEFR's illustrative scales include such tasks as informal conversation, formal discussions, transactions for obtaining goods and services, and goal-oriented cooperation. For our purposes, we will focus on the global descriptors of speakers at levels B2, C1, and C2 as well as descriptors for formal discussions.

Qualities of spoken language, according to the CEFR scale, include range, accuracy, fluency, interaction, and coherence. Range most readily corresponds to ACTFL's concept of "global tasks and functions." It refers to the breadth of linguistic resources available to a learner and his or her ability to flexibly use those resources. Like Novice learners, according to the ACTFL scale, A1 learners have "a very basic repertoire of words related to personal details and particular concrete situations." At C2, speakers can use their lexical and syntactic repertoire flexibly and convey subtle shades of meaning. CEFR guidelines define accuracy in much the same way that ACTFL guidelines do, except that no specific grammatical features are specified in any of the scales. By the time a speaker reaches the B2 range, his or her mistakes do not interfere with communication. At the C1 and C2 levels, grammatical mistakes are "rare" and "difficult to spot." Fluency has no direct correlate in the ACTFL descriptors. This criterion describes the extent to which learners are able to express themselves fluidly and effortlessly. Coherence, to some extent, reflects ACTFL's focus on "text types." It concerns learners' ability to create cohesive discourse by making appropriate use of a wide range of organizational patterns, connectors, and other devices. Finally, interaction refers to learners' ability to engage with native speakers in culturally appropriate ways. It includes, among other things, knowing how to initiate and manage conversations and negotiate meaning with other people as well as knowing what sorts of body language, eye contact, and proximity to other people are appropriate.

A learner at B2 is often described as a "vantage speaker." Speakers at this level can operate quite independently and are able to interact with native speakers easily, without too much strain for either of them. In many countries, a learner who has reached B2 is capable of working in native firms in most areas of specialty. At the B2 level, a speaker's range is sufficient to give clear descriptions and express viewpoints on most general topics without much conspicuous searching for words and using some complex forms to do so. Speakers at this level demonstrate a relatively high degree of grammatical control; they do not make errors that cause misunderstanding. They are able to produce stretches of language with a fairly even tempo with few noticeably long pauses. In terms of interactional competence, they can initiate discourse, take turns when appropriate, and end conversations as necessary, though these may not always be done elegantly. Speakers at this level can facilitate discussion on familiar ground, confirming understanding, inviting others to participate, and so on. In terms of coherence, learners at the B2 level use a limited number of cohesive devices to link their utterances into clear, coherent discourse.

At C2, learners are considered "proficient." Their range is broad, allowing them to select formulations to express themselves clearly and in an appropriate style on a wide range of topics. Errors at this level are rare, difficult to spot, and generally corrected by the learner when they occur. Only conceptually difficult subjects can hinder the natural, smooth flow of language for a C2 speaker. Learners at this level are also able to skillfully preface their remarks in order to get or keep the floor and to relate their own contributions to those of other speakers. Their speech is characterized by controlled use of organizational patterns, connectors, and cohesive devices.

Owing to their range, C2 learners enjoy great linguistic flexibility, sufficient to convey subtle shades of meaning precisely, to give emphasis, and to eliminate ambiguity. In terms of accuracy, C2 speakers maintain a high control of complex language. They express themselves with a natural colloquial fluency. In terms of interaction, such learners interact with ease and skill, picking up on and using nonverbal and intonational cues effortlessly. The coherence of their speech is such that they make full and appropriate use of a sophisticated range of organizational patterns and a wide range of connectors and other cohesive devices.

Both the ACTFL and the CEFR guidelines indicate that Advanced-level learners of a language must be able to argue viewpoints and convey their messages using sophisticated language, tailored to the audience. It is precisely these areas of proficiency that written persuasive essays and oral debates target. In the remainder of this document, we will reference the ACTFL guidelines, which are more familiar to American audiences.

2

Task-Based Language Learning

Definition

Simply put, a task is "an activity conducted in the foreign language that results in a product with a measurable result such that students can determine for themselves whether or not they have adequately completed the assignment" (Leaver and Kaplan 2004, 47). From an outcomes perspective, a task reflects an activity that requires learners "to arrive at an outcome from given information through some processes of thought" and that allows teachers "to control and regulate that process" (Prabhu 1987, 2). Additionally, some tasks involve goal-oriented activities aimed at accomplishing a concrete outcome, such as doing a puzzle or playing a game, and push learners to use whatever target language resources they have in order to solve a given problem (Willis 1996, 53).

Background

Debate in the foreign language classroom enables language to become a vehicle for communicating ideas for meaningful purposes rather than functioning solely as an object of study (Coyle, Hood, and Marsh 2010; van Lier 2005; Long 2007; Stryker and Leaver 1997; MLA Ad Hoc Committee 2007; Shaw 1997; Hedegaard 2005). Because competing positions evolve during the course of a debate, learners must pay careful attention to ongoing exchanges. In such a meaning-focused task, participants "are not simply displaying their control of particular patterns or structures or phrases, which would be a linguistic objective" (Willis 2004, 13). Rather, they are constructing meaning for a real purpose in order to learn the language. Likewise, debate forces learners to "push their linguistic competence to its limit as they attempt to express their ideas" (Swain 1993, 162) and negotiate meaning. Research conducted by J. Massie (2005) and Ulla Connor (1987) identifies the task of argumentation and debate as a valuable strategy for improving both L2 oral and written proficiency, particularly at the Advanced level.

In Practice

Incorporating debate in the foreign language classroom can take on many forms, and one is not necessarily better than another. Rather than adopting a one-size-fits-all method, program dynamics (e.g., open versus selective enrollment and proficiency testing) should factor into choosing a suitable approach.

Open versus Selective Enrollment

Both enrollment approaches have advantages and disadvantages that should be weighed carefully. The obvious advantage to an open-enrollment course is that it does not discriminate by proficiency; however, making such a course available to any upper-division student can result in a wide range of proficiencies in a single language class and, hence, create considerable imbalance. The cognitive aspect of debate reflects an Advanced-level task and, correspondingly, those possessing an Advanced level of language proficiency tend to benefit the most from such an approach. If you wish to establish a set of criteria by which students are rated on a selective-enrollment basis, here are some suggestions:

1. Require participants to complete pre- and post-OPIs, either by telephone or via computer (OPIc), and a written proficiency test. We also recommend testing for reading and listening.
2. Require applicants to complete a background questionnaire that elicits information about applicants' prior language experience, professional goals, motivation for learning a foreign language, and so on.

Proficiency Testing

Whether or not you intend to allow open enrollment, we recommend some form of pre-testing to establish students' proficiency levels. ACTFL's OPI is widely accepted and used, but it may be prohibitively expensive. The new computer-based OPI (OPIc) is much more cost effective and easier to administer, but its highest rating is Advanced (without regard to sublevels). The Computer Oral Proficiency Interview developed by the Center for Applied Linguistics (as of this writing, available only for Arabic and Spanish) is a similar semi-adaptive test of oral proficiency. Those who buy the test also receive a rater training module to help them rate student performance.

A variety of self-assessment options are also available. ACTFL has released its own "Can-Do Statements" tied to its proficiency guidelines. These are a series of statements that allow learners to evaluate what they are capable of doing with the language. For instance, a typical statement at the Superior level relates to presentational communication: "I can deliver detailed presentations with accuracy, clarity, and precision to a wide variety of audiences on topics ranging from broad general interests to areas of specialized expertise."[6] Similarly, the CEFR has a self-assessment grid for each of its six levels. A typical C2 statement for written production includes a profile like the following: "I can write clear, smoothly flowing text in an appropriate style. I can write complex letters, reports or articles, which present a case with an effective logical structure, which helps the recipient to notice and remember significant points. I can write summaries and reviews of professional or literary works."[7] LinguaFolio, developed by the University of Oregon, is yet another option. Unlike ACTFL and CEFR, LinguaFolio represents more than just a series of can-do statements. Instead, it is a portfolio for language learners that comprises three components: self-assessments, biographical information, and a dossier that contains samples of the learner's work. The self-assessments comprise a series of checklists in which students answer whether or not they can perform certain tasks explicitly tied to the ACTFL proficiency guidelines. For example, learners respond to "I can give and seek personal views and opinions on a variety of familiar topics." LinguaFolio is free, making it cost effective and time efficient (for teachers), but its dependence on self-assessment may make the instrument less reliable.

ACTFL is currently developing reading and listening tests for a number of languages, including Arabic, Chinese, English, French, German, Russian, Spanish, and Turkish, which are tied to ACTFL proficiency guidelines using a criterion-referenced approach (Clifford and Cox 2013). Such tests will contribute valuable information about a learner's overall language profile and at a reasonable cost.

Understandably, ACTFL testing or equivalent pre- and post-testing may not be options for everyone, particularly for an open-enrollment course, nor is it essential in order to carry out an advanced foreign language course through debate. However, regardless of the selection process, we recommend some form of pre- and post-testing since pre-test ratings provide a useful benchmark by which to gauge possible gains as measured by post-testing carried out at the end of the course.

In order to help students understand what constitutes a language learner in any of the modalities at the Advanced and Superior levels, consider distributing a copy of the ACTFL or related proficiency guidelines to all participants at the beginning of the semester. The earlier-mentioned Can-Do statements also enable students to self-assess their language skills.[8] With proficiency guidelines, self-assessment findings, and—circumstances permitting—pre-OPI and written proficiency test ratings in hand, participants are able both to pinpoint their strengths and weaknesses and target specific areas on which to focus.

Class Size

Naturally, for an open-enrollment course, class size will vary and such fluctuations can serve as an opportunity to explore different methods. In addition to sheer numbers, consider whether enrollment numbers are even or odd. Take, for example, a course comprising seven students. From a functional standpoint, having seven students facilitates the creation of two teams of three (six total) with one alternate in the event of an absence. From a pedagogical standpoint, having an alternate facilitates a system of rotating peer reviewers / judges. Fessenden and colleagues (1973, 254) recommend that reviewers judge a team's "maintenance of goals, the clarity of the discussion, the effectiveness of the leadership, the fullness with which opposing points of view are elaborated, the blockages that occur in the group's thinking, [and] breakdowns in any aspect of the group process. It is usually desirable for all members to share the responsibility for appraising the operation of the group. The rotation of the function tends to focus the attention of all members on strengths and weaknesses and contributes to more efficient group functioning." Thus, students carry out the roles both of active debater and critical observer. So what might otherwise seem problematic can, in fact, prove valuable and instructive if leveraged properly.

Drawing on the aforementioned model of two teams of three, participants could have seven minutes each to present for or against a claim (forty-two minutes total), thus allowing time for post-debate discussion and evaluation. We recommend using this time, while the debate and topic-specific vocabulary are still very much on the minds of participants, to point out both successful and unsuccessful attempts at applying lexical items introduced in the given chapter. If limited to a fifty-minute class period and if class size exceeds six, consider reducing the number of minutes allotted to each student. Alternatively, if class size becomes excessively large, consider meeting as an entire class in preparation for the culminating debate but creating four debate teams and holding two simultaneous debates in separate rooms.

Cross-Cultural Dimensions of Debate

In his seminal work titled *Rhetoric*, Aristotle established a rhetorical tradition that has and continues to permeate Western civilization. However, his objective in writing *Rhetoric* "was not to describe Greek rhetoric, but to describe this universal facet of human communication" (Kennedy 1984, 10). Indeed, one can look to Eastern civilization and likewise find long-established rhetorical traditions.[9]

As a point of departure, this volume and, by extension, the ACTFL and CEFR oral proficiency guidelines outlined earlier reflect the Greek rhetorical tradition, but we want to emphasize the interrelatedness of language and culture, particularly at the Advanced level and beyond, and as such encourage sensitivity toward and respect for nuanced aspects of debate specific to a language and its culture. Among English-speaking nations, one finds varying stylistic and methodological approaches to debate, for example, British versus American debating traditions.[10] Ultimately the approaches set forth in this volume aim to transcend national and international boundaries and facilitate a global dialogue.

3

Teaching Reading

WE START WITH READING because reading plays a fundamental role in preparing learners for their tasks; in order to effectively complete the tasks, learners must become familiar with the topic and the issues related to it and must learn the requisite vocabulary.

Proficiency Guidelines for Reading

Choose texts based on the ACTFL proficiency guidelines (*ACTFL Proficiency Guidelines 2012*). The guidelines both indicate what readers must be able to do and describe the kinds of texts that readers should be able to handle. For purposes of a course on debate, select editorials on controversial topics that may require the learner to make inferences.

Research on Reading

Reading plays an important role in language learning. Not only is it an important skill that must be acquired for its own sake, it is also a necessary means by which learners can develop their overall linguistic competence. Reading textual information in a target language provides input and lasting, easily retrievable models of language structures. At the Novice and Intermediate levels of language learning, the focus of reading instruction is often on learning to read. As students become more advanced in their skills, the focus shifts to reading to learn. Reading to learn becomes particularly important for Advanced-level learners, who, as Leaver and Shekht-man (2002) note, become more interested in *what* to say than *how*. In courses structured around debate and other Advanced-level language functions, texts not only provide learners with authentic input and language models but also provide them with important content information. Through written texts, learners can become acquainted with conceptual issues related to the assigned topics, familiarize themselves with the arguments on both sides of the issue—in addition to learning the specialized vocabulary that attends each topic—and observe common structures for offering and countering opinions.

Research on reading demonstrates that a number of factors affect learners' ability to comprehend written texts. As generally acknowledged by the research, these factors can be categorized as either *reader-based factors* (e.g., background knowledge, linguistic knowledge, and strategic knowledge) or *text-based factors* (e.g., discourse organization and vocabulary).

Background Knowledge

Ample evidence suggests that a reader's background knowledge plays an important role in reading comprehension (Bernhardt 2005). Background knowledge includes all the experiences that a reader brings to a text: life experiences, educational experiences, knowledge of how texts are organized, and so on. Background knowledge, which also may be referred to as *schema* in the reading literature, helps learners anticipate the discourse organization of the text and disambiguate word-level and clausal meanings. Some learners may have little to no prior knowledge of a particular topic. In such cases, the instructor must establish the background knowledge necessary for the learners to comprehend the text.

Linguistic Knowledge

Learners' proficiency in their L2 plays an important role in their ability to comprehend written texts. In the research literature on reading, the debate has often centered on the question of whether learners' first language (L1) reading skills or their L2 proficiency plays a more important role in comprehension. Clarke's (1980) language threshold hypothesis posits that L2 readers must have sufficient L2 knowledge in order to efficiently apply their L1 reading strategies and skills to comprehending an L2 text. As Grabe and Stoller (2011, 43) put it, "If readers are devoting most of their cognitive resources to figuring out the language of the L2 text, there are few cognitive resources left over for the fluent comprehension processes that would normally support the L1 reader." Many researchers believe that only after learners reach advanced levels of L2 proficiency can L1 reading ability make a difference (see Bernhardt 2001; Grabe 2009).

Of particular importance to reading comprehension is the size of the reader's vocabulary (Laufer 1997; Pulido and Hambrick 2008). Evidence suggests that if students are to understand a wide range of texts with adequate comprehension, they need to recognize at least 95 percent of the words that they might encounter in these texts, and greater comprehension generally occurs when a reader recognizes 98 to 99 percent of the words in a given text (Laufer and Ravenhorst-Kalovski 2010; Nation 2006). Thus, vocabulary instruction is an important element for improving reading comprehension.

Strategic Knowledge

A reader's ability to monitor his or her own reading plays an essential role in successful comprehension. This ability allows readers to decide whether they are achieving their intended purpose and to adjust their actions to improve understanding. Research suggests that teaching learners specific metacognitive skills—"thinking about thinking"—has a positive impact on the reader's comprehension process (see reviews by Anderson 2005).

Readability (Text-Based Factors)

While reader-based factors such as background knowledge and L2 proficiency play vital roles in reading comprehension, the readability of the text itself can also influence the reading process. A text's readability is influenced by a number of variables, including discourse organization, vocabulary, length, content, and interest level.

Discourse Organization

Research has shown that students retain and remember information best when texts are presented in an organized way (e.g., comparison/contrast, problem/solution, and cause/effect; see Meyer 1987). Another aspect of text structure found to play a key role in comprehension is the use of signaling cues or features. Signaling cues are words or phrases that explicitly state the main idea (e.g., "the main issue at hand is . . . "), or demonstrate connections between ideas (e.g., "on the other hand . . ."), or reveal the organizational development (e.g., "as mentioned above"). Nonlinguistic signaling features in a printed text include charts, graphs, pictures, diagrams, and maps as well as structural organizers such as titles, subtitles, and numbering of sections.

Vocabulary

The vocabulary used in a particular text also plays an important role in the learner's ability to understand. Word frequency—both the frequency with which a word is repeated in the text itself and the frequency with which a particular word appears in the language—can influence comprehension. Metaphorical language, in which words are not used in their traditional sense, can pose problems for learners. Additionally, the "transparency" of the vocabulary (see Bransford and Johnson 1972) is a factor; explicit definitions are normally easier to understand than implicit ones. In addition, the number of propositions and features such as pronoun references or narrative voice may affect comprehension.

Length

The length of texts that students are asked to read can affect comprehension. Recent studies suggest that longer texts may actually be easier for students to comprehend as they are more cohesive and generally provide more context to facilitate meaning making (Gascoigne 2002; Maxim 2002; Swaffar and Arens 2005). Jane Swaffar and Katherine Arens suggest that texts of five hundred words or more help activate effective reading strategies.

Content and Interest Level of the Text

The extent to which the content of a text captures readers' interests may also affect comprehension. In a study by Veronica Dristas and G. Grisenti (1995, cited in Shrum and Glisan 2010), students read two L2 texts. One was judged to be linguistically less challenging but also less interesting than the other. However, student comprehension was greater when students were reading text they found more interesting. Thus, in selecting texts, it is important to choose texts that are relevant to the learners.

Scaffolding the Reading Process

To help learners succeed in reading, we suggest adhering to several principles taken from researchers such as Grabe and Stoller (2011) and Anderson and Han (2009): (1) activate the learners' prior knowledge in appropriate ways, (2) build vocabulary, (3) teach comprehension, (4) improve reading fluency, (5) develop strategic readers, and (6) encourage extensive reading. These principles are based on extensive review of the L2 reading research. (See Grabe and Stoller [2011] and Anderson and Han [2009] for a more extensive overview of principles underlying reading instruction.) Note that many of these same principles undergird listening comprehension, and some of the same techniques may be applied by instructors when teaching learners listening. Moreover, the principles underlying vocabulary acquisition benefit speaking and writing as well as listening and reading.

Activate Prior Knowledge

As demonstrated earlier, background knowledge is one of the most important factors affecting the reading process. A significant amount of research suggests that reading comprehension and reading skills are significantly improved when prior knowledge is activated. Below we list several techniques for activating learners' prior knowledge.

VISUALS
Pictures and other visual material can help to activate learners' prior knowledge. For instance, a picture of an oil spill in the ocean can bring to mind past oil spills, the consequences of oil spills, the causes of oil spills, and so on. Learners may be asked to look at pictures and then brainstorm all of the topics that come to mind.

PRE-READING DISCUSSIONS
Pre-reading discussions provide an opportunity for readers to determine what they know about a topic and what others may know. Students about to discuss income inequality, for example, might be asked, "To what extent do you think quality of life differs for the rich and the poor?" These discussions can be held in smaller groups or can be led by the teacher. A think/pair/share (in which learners are given a minute or two to think silently before sharing with a neighbor and then engaging in a whole-class discussion) or a jot/pair/share (a variation of a think/pair/share in which learners

are directed to jot down their ideas before they begin a discussion) may be appropriate at the beginning of this activity.

KNOW, WANT TO KNOW, LEARNED CHART
A Know, Want to Know, Learned (KWL) chart comprising three columns is commonly used for promoting strategic reading and motivating students to read by having them discover what they have learned from the reading. Before reading a text, learners list in the first column what they *know* (K), followed by in the second column what they *want* (W) to know from a text before they read. Once they have finished reading, they list in the third column what they have *learned* (L) from the reading. A simple KWL chart can be made on the board or distributed as a handout.

ANTICIPATION GUIDE
Similar to a KWL chart is an anticipation or reaction guide. Anticipation guides contain a series of statements related to the topic or point of view of a particular text. The purpose of the guide is to learn what readers already know about the topic of the reading.

Prepare several key statements related to the content of a reading passage. If you are trying to develop the readers' ability to make inferences, prepare five (or more) inference statements. Before the students read the passage, they read the inference statements and determine whether they agree or disagree with them. The students then read the passage and respond a second time to the same inference statements. Table 1 includes an anticipation guide dealing with the right to privacy.

ATTENTION TO TEXT STRUCTURE
A pre-reading discussion on the type of text structure and what expectations a reader may have about the organization of the material is very valuable for L2 readers. Learners could be directed to look at the title, pictures, headings, graphs, and so on. They can be directed to discuss the kinds of transition or linking words they expect to find based on the type of text. A narrative, for instance, will make much more use of sequential markers while a comparison will use a different set of vocabulary.

DIRECTED READING-THINKING ACTIVITY
A directed reading-thinking activity (DR-TA) can be used as part of the pre-reading process but also during reading. A DR-TA guides students in asking questions about a text, making predictions, and then reading to

Table 1. Anticipation Guide

Before reading the text, read through each of the statements below. Write "A" if you agree with the statement or "D" if you disagree. Then read the text. After reading it, reread the statements below to see if your views have changed. Write "A" if you agree with the statement or "D" if you disagree.

Response before Reading	Statement	Response after Reading
	1. The right to privacy is an absolute right.	
	2. Privacy is the right to be left alone.	
	3. The government does not have the right to violate the privacy of its citizens.	

Note: To download a PDF of the illustrations in this book, please visit http://press.georgetown.edu/book/languages/teaching-advanced-language-skills-through-global-debate.

confirm their predictions. First, learners make predictions about what they think is coming next, then they read to prove or disprove their predications, and then they discuss their predictions and reformulate them, using what they have learned before moving on.

Before using a DR-TA, read the text and determine appropriate pause points, that is, points where you will stop to ask the reader, "What do you think the author may mention next?" Below are some commonly used questions adapted for opinion pieces:

1. What arguments do you predict the author will use?
2. What are your reasons for these predictions?
3. What do you think now?
4. What made you change your mind?
5. Can you find information in the text to support or challenge your predictions?
6. Do you want to revise your predictions?
7. Why do you want to revise your predictions? What hints did the author give you?
8. What do you think the author will do next to convince his or her reader?

Build Vocabulary

As mentioned earlier, vocabulary knowledge is crucial for reading comprehension, with scholars claiming that students must be able to understand

95 percent of the words in a text—for most texts, that figure lies somewhere between ten thousand and fifteen thousand words—in order to avoid frustration (Schmitt 2008). Norbert Schmitt further suggests that learners need explicit or intentional study of vocabulary rather than the incidental study that typically happens in classrooms. Moreover, learners need direct vocabulary practice with large sets of words. In the following we list a variety of methods for vocabulary learning, though this list is by no means exhaustive.

Concept-of-Definition Map for Introducing New Vocabulary

One way to introduce a new key word is to connect it to what learners already know. This can be accomplished by "building" a concept-of-definition map. In this approach, students view a key word from four vantage points: the definition of the word, its characteristics, examples, and nonexamples. (See figure 1 for an example.)

Word Structure Analysis

Research in English as a second language shows that teaching students common morphological endings facilitates word comprehension (Graves et al.

Figure 1: Concept of Definition Map

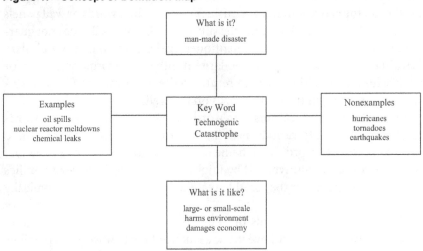

Note: To download a PDF of the illustrations in this book, please visit http://press.georgetown.edu/book/languages/teaching-advanced-language-skills-through-global-debate.

2012). Moreover, learning vocabulary through incidental exposure (reading and listening) is more effective when students know how to attend to new language, including knowing how to use a dictionary and how to recognize contextual clues, but also by being aware of word families and affixes in order to analyze words by their parts. Thus, teachers should encourage learners to study prefixes, roots, and suffixes and use this knowledge to learn new vocabulary. Teachers should help learners to recognize parts of a word, which is best accomplished by breaking them into their components. Learners should also memorize the meaning of prefixes and roots. Moreover, learners must learn to combine prefixes and roots to create words, and to recognize how combined meanings work together to create new word meanings (see Nation 1990).

In addition to word analysis, other tasks that can help students intentionally learn new vocabulary include locating selected words in the text, matching definitions to new words, producing derivatives of words to create other parts of speech in word families, replacing underlined words in sentences with similar words from the text, and arranging words into sentences (Paribakht and Wesche 1996, 1997). Many of these activities can be accomplished by making use of word walls, which we discuss next.

Word Walls

When possible, teachers can create a vocabulary-rich environment by displaying key words and phrases from core readings on bulletin boards or on posters on the classroom walls. Consider color-coding words or wall panels to assist with learning. However, the simple display of words does not guarantee vocabulary learning. As mentioned earlier, intentional vocabulary learning is necessary to learn the large numbers of words necessary for successful reading. The key is to return to the word wall and engage students in meaningful use of the words on the walls.

One way to engage learners with words is to have them cluster the words on the word wall into various meaningful groups. For instance, they could categorize words according to theme or connotation (positive or negative) or synonyms and antonyms. They might group words into word families or by parts of speech, or they might create collocations (words that typically occur together).

Beyond categorizing words on the word walls, learners can engage in speed writes in which they have to use as many of the new words as possible, design crossword puzzles, rank activities, carry out spontaneous speaking tasks, or conduct role plays.

Spaced Repetition: Memory Boxes

Students learning new vocabulary typically engage in massed repetition of words, in which they make a list of vocabulary on a single sheet of paper, fold the paper in half, and then write a definition (or translation) opposite the vocabulary. Studying vocabulary this way is usually crammed into a short period of time. While this technique may be effective for quick, short-term learning, the words are usually quickly lost from memory, typically after a vocabulary test. Spaced repetition is much more effective at developing long-term memory. Software programs such as the free Anki (also available as an app for mobile devices) allow instructors and learners to build individualized flashcards and select intervals for repetition. The Sample Memory Box Card below depicts another method of spaced repetition.

The numbers in the top left corner, 1 through 7, represent days of the week. The numbers in the center, 1 through 4, represent weeks in a month, and the final set of numbers represents the months. Students review new memory card items every day for a week and cross off each number on the left as they go to track their progress. After reviewing a set of items for a week, they review them one time per week for a month, this time crossing off the numbers in the center as they go. After reviewing the items one time per week for a month, they review them one time per month for a year, or at least for the duration of the course. Consider using different color cards for different types of words, including connecting words, idioms, topic-specific lexical items / phrases, or words based on a particular root.

Sample Memory Box Card (Russian-English)

1 2 3 4 5 6 7   1 2 3 4   1 2 3 4 5 6 7 8 9 10 11 12

В ка́ждой шу́тке есть до́ля пра́вды—Many a true word is spoken in jest
Терпе́ние и труд всё перетру́т—Nothing is impossible to a willing mind
У дурака́ до́лго де́ньги не де́ржатся—A fool and his money are soon
    parted
Цыпля́т по о́сени счита́ют—Don't count your chickens before they
    are hatched

Teach Comprehension

Often teachers give more attention to testing reading comprehension than they do to teaching learners how to process what they are reading. Learners must develop and practice comprehension skills and be taught how to monitor their understanding.

Questioning Strategies

A common practice for assessing reading comprehension is the use of post-reading comprehension questions. Grabe and Stoller (2011) suggest that post-reading questions can lead to effective instruction in comprehension skills if teachers ask students to (1) explain why an answer is appropriate, (2) point out where the text supports their answers, or (3) engage in a discussion about how to understand the text better. In addition, teachers can engage learners in classroom conversations in which they identify and explore main ideas in the texts they are reading, noting how information connects across parts of the text, building linkages between two or more readings, and promoting connections between ideas in the texts and student background knowledge. Post-reading questions can provide a valuable starting point for such class discussions, but students must be invited to follow up on their initial responses with further elaboration.

During Reading Activities

In order for learners to improve their reading comprehension of texts, they must become aware of text structure and discourse organization while reading. Textbooks often do not include activities to be done during reading, so teachers can create them to guide students' reading and draw their attention to text organization features. Depending on the nature of the text, teachers can ask students to do any of the following while reading:

1. Complete an outline of the text that reveals the main units of the text. This outline may be partially complete. As part of the post-reading discussion, students can explain how they identified each unit as a separate unit.
2. Fill in a graphic organizer, such as those pictured in appendix A. When reading position papers, learners can write out the arguments, along with any counterarguments mentioned. As part of post-reading, stu-

dents can share their completed graphs and explain how the information in the graphic was signaled in the text.

3. Underline clues that indicate major patterns of organization (e.g., cause and effect, comparison and contrast, problem and solution).

4. Highlight transition phrases and signal words that indicate new sections. During the post-reading discussion, students can describe what the phrases and words signal.

5. Assign a brief main idea label to each paragraph (or set of paragraphs) in the margin. During the discussion after the reading, students can compare margin notes and explore how each paragraph functions within the whole.

6. Summarize a reading passage or a partial passage after the reading. Summaries help learners distinguish between the main ideas, supporting ideas, and details of a text. A successful summary demonstrates that a reader recognizes the differences among these different levels and can place emphasis at the proper level.

Teaching Students to Ask Questions

Studies suggest that effective readers often ask questions about what they are reading as they are reading. Learners should be invited and taught to ask questions of their own, especially during reading. Students may be instructed to identify challenging portions of a text and to formulate questions about material they do not understand and about which they would like to seek clarification. Through a class discussion, the teacher can guide students to identify the source of the difficulty and strategies for overcoming the challenges. Often the first step in teaching for comprehension is to ask readers to identify what they do not comprehend—and why.

QUESTIONING THE AUTHOR

Questioning the author (QtA) is another method designed to teach students to ask questions. This approach, developed by Isabel Beck and colleagues (1997), assists students with constructing meaning from a text and is meant to be carried out during reading, rather than after reading. The approach requires the teacher to model an effective reading behavior: asking questions in order to make sense of a text.

To use this approach, read the selected text, deciding on pause points, where you think students need to stop, think, and gain a deeper understanding of the text. Next create questions that can be asked of students at each pause point to encourage higher order thinking as well as to draw their attention to discourse structure and other features. Sample questions include:

1. What is the author trying to say?
2. What is the author's message?
3. Why does the author choose to include this particular information?
4. Do you think the author's message is clear? Why or why not?
5. How could the author say this more clearly?
6. What types of examples could have been added to strengthen the author's position?
7. Do the author's examples help or create some confusion?
8. How does the author signal main ideas?
9. Are the author's main ideas clearly stated and explained?
10. Did the author give us the answer to the issue that he or she has raised?
11. What biases or perspectives does the author reveal?
12. What is the significance of the author's message?

In early stages, QtA is guided and modeled by the teacher, with the ultimate goal being that learners can use these techniques when reading on their own.

ELABORATIVE INTERROGATION

Elaborative interrogation is a type of comprehension questioning that centers on follow-up "why" questions that oblige students to return to the text, reread, and then explain their answers. In this technique, learners read a simple factual statement and then turn the statement into a "why" question, which they must answer by returning to the text. For example, students might read a statement like, "In industrialized nations, emissions contribute to increased respiratory illnesses." Students would then rephrase this as a "why" question—"Why would industrialization contribute to health problems?"—and either use their background knowledge or information from the text to answer this question. Initially the teacher should guide elaborative interrogation in a class discussion. The goal is for learners to use this technique while engaging with the text on their own.

Improve Reading Fluency

Why Consider Fluency?

Fluent reading—rapid and accurate—is often ignored in most L2 reading curricula (Grabe and Stoller 2011). However, most reading research has demonstrated that reading fluency is a critical component of effective and successful reading instruction (Grabe 2009). Reading speed may seem unimportant, but it does indeed play an important role in comprehension. Readers who struggle to decode words or to access their meanings cannot develop an accurate understanding of the text as a whole.

Even highly bilingual readers read at a rate "30% or more slower than L1 reading rates" (Segalowitz, Poulsen, and Komoda 1991). Linda Jensen (1986, 106) indicates that "at the end of a [reading] course, even advanced L2 students may read only 100 words per minute or less," much less than an average of 250 to 300 words per minute of skilled L1 readers. Thus, to improve reading comprehension, instructors should devote time to activities designed to build fluency. A number of such activities are described below.

Shadow Reading

Shadow reading provides a structured opportunity for learners to read fluently. First teachers should find an audio recording of the text they plan to use in class or read it out loud themselves. Learners first listen to the passage without reading along. Following the listening passage, they discuss what they heard.

Next, after a brief discussion, readers look at the text and follow along silently as they listen to the text. Most of the learners' eyes will move faster following the text while listening than if they focus solely on the text without listening. This helps them to develop reading fluency.

Finally, learners read aloud quietly along with the recording. Keeping up may be a challenge, as learners are not accustomed to reading quickly out loud. Following the shadow reading activity, learners will answer reading comprehension questions that accompany the passage (or have been created for the passage).

Rate Buildup Reading

Students are given sixty seconds to read a passage as quickly (and as accurately) as they can. After the sixty-second period, learners are given an additional sixty seconds to read the same passage from the beginning; they are to read more material during the second reading than during the first. This process should be repeated at least three to four times total. Such an activity helps learners to move their eyes faster as they read over "old" material. However, it is important to keep the focus on comprehension so learners actually process the material they are reading.

Repeated Reading

Students read a short passage over and over again until they achieve predetermined comprehension and reading rates. For instance, you might ask learners to read a one hundred–word paragraph four times in two minutes. This technique has been shown to improve reading fluency (Samuels 1979).

Oral Paired Reading

This technique, while frequently used in L1 settings to build fluency, is rarely used in L2 classrooms. Like the repeated reading task described earlier, students read a text with which they are very familiar, out loud to a partner.

Class-Paced Reading

This activity may begin with setting a class goal for a minimal reading rate. Once that goal is established, calculate the average number of words per page in a particular reading assignment, then decide how much material the students have to read within one minute in order to reach their goal. For example, if the goal is to read 250 words per minute, and the average page contains 250 words, then the goal should be to read one page every minute. If the page has 500 words, then the students should read half of a page every sixty seconds, and a quarter of a page every thirty seconds. This may also be done by number of lines, calculating average number of words per line. Students may then mark off chunks of text. Direct the students to begin reading the material. After thirty seconds (or sixty seconds) has elapsed, indicate to the class that they should move to the next page or the next section in the reading. Students who read faster are not expected to slow down their reading.

Self-Paced Reading

Self-paced reading is similar to the class-based procedure described earlier, except that students determine their own goals and how much material they must read to meet their objectives. As with the previous exercise, direct the students to move on at intervals of thirty seconds to one minute apart.

Rereading (Different from Repeated Reading)

Rereading of familiar texts represents one of the best ways to improve reading fluency. Instructors rarely require that learners reread material, but giving students a reason to read the text again will benefit both comprehension and reading rate. In designing reading activities, teachers should consider asking students to read texts multiple times, each time with a different purpose in mind. Some potential purposes are listed below:

1. Confirm the main idea (skim)
2. Locate details (scan)
3. Prepare for a summary or synthesis task
4. Read between the lines (inferencing)
5. Fill in a graphic organizer that reflects text organization
6. Prepare for a follow-up activity requiring use of text information (e.g., radio report, essay, debate, or play)
7. Confirm answers to comprehension questions
8. Determine the author's stance, bias, and position
9. Locate text structure signals, main idea signals
10. Find points of disagreement with another information source (text, lecture, video)

Develop Strategic Learners

Strategies are conscious actions taken by learners to improve their reading comprehension. Research suggests that successful readers are able to successfully orchestrate the use of a variety of strategies to improve their reading outcomes (see Anderson 2005 for an overview). Yet many L2 readers do not make use of strategies or do not effectively use the strategies that are available to them. For this reason researchers suggest that the teacher should teach strategies explicitly through modeling followed by practice on the part of the learners. A number of the main idea comprehension techniques described earlier are designed to help learners ask questions about the reading—an important comprehension strategy. Here we highlight the importance of "thinking aloud" while reading, and we cite Anderson's (2005) suggestions for using think-aloud techniques in the reading classroom.

1. Model the use of thinking aloud by first selecting a passage that you have never read before. Read the passage aloud while the learners follow along silently. While reading, verbally report your thoughts about the passage. For instance, "I haven't seen this word before, but since the sentence is about pollution, I'm going to guess that the word means X." Or, perhaps, "It seems like the author is telling me that

something bad is going to happen. I predict that there will be an accident."

2. At the conclusion of the demonstration, ask the students to add any thoughts that occurred to them during the reading.
3. If necessary, provide additional demonstrations.
4. Divide students into groups of two or three and have them work together to practice reading aloud. One student reads aloud while the others follow along. Encourage learners to verbalize their thoughts and the strategies they use while reading along.
5. The students who were listening then share with their peers what they were thinking during the process.
6. This activity can also be done in a "reading round robin" mode, in which each student reads aloud one sentence at a time and then verbalizes thoughts and strategies.
7. This strategy can be used in silent reading periods. After directing learners to read silently for a period, stop them and ask what they are thinking.
8. Consider asking students to practice this activity while reading outside of the classroom and to discuss their successes in class.

This technique helps learners become more aware of what they are doing while they are reading and to see what other readers do when they encounter difficulties. Modeling strategies with students and then giving them opportunities for practice is an effective way to teach other strategies, including some of the following:

1. Set a purpose for reading. Generally we recommend that teachers set a purpose for reading and that they clearly communicate that purpose to the learners before asking them to read a difficult text. When readers have a purpose, they find it easier to focus their attention. Reading to find the main idea requires very different levels of attention than reading to criticize an argument.

   Even though we recommend that instructors set a clear purpose for reading, learners can benefit from setting their own purposes, especially for any reading they do on their own. To set a purpose, learners can ask themselves questions like the following: (1) What is the author's purpose in this piece?; (2) What questions do I hope will be answered?; (3) Why am I reading this text?; and (4) What do I hope to do with the information I glean from this text? Note that a KWL chart is particularly useful in this regard as it both activates background knowledge and focuses the learners on their reading purposes.

2. Synthesize along the way. Teach students to stop periodically, look away from the text, and summarize in their own words what they have read. Writing a sentence or two of summary may also prove useful for learners. This technique can help readers to process information and to avoid overload. It also ascertains whether learners are actively constructing meaning or passively moving their eyes across the page. This technique can also serve to help learners monitor their comprehension. If they are unable to summarize what they have read, then they have not understood and may need to reread.

3. Ask questions. Several of the techniques suggested earlier, such as DR-TA, QtA, and Elaborative Interrogation, use questions to help learners clarify meaning and probe for deeper understanding.

4. Create visual structures or graphic organizers. Among the graphic organizers that readers may wish to use are maps, chains, charts, webs, trees, matrices, and diagrams. Each of these techniques provides visual representations of a text's structure in order to facilitate comprehension. By delineating the key parts of a text and the relationship among its parts, organizers help learners identify the most important ideas.

Extensive Reading

The term "extensive reading" was originally coined by Palmer (1968), to distinguish it from "intensive reading"—the careful reading of texts for detailed comprehension and skills practice. Extensive reading involves the reading of large amounts of easily understood material, usually done outside of class and at each student's pace and level, and is believed to facilitate vocabulary acquisition (Nation 1997) as well as promote learners' motivation (Powell 2005). Few, if any, follow-up exercises are assigned because the aim is for overall understanding rather than detailed analysis. For the same reason, dictionaries are used minimally. Above all, the reading should be enjoyable.

An ambitious teacher may seek out reading material related to the debate topics to share with students, either in paper form or online. This approach allows the teacher to control the difficulty of the texts and to ensure that none are beyond the level of the students. Another approach involves allowing students to choose articles on their own. For instance, a teacher might assign learners to read one article related to the topic of discussion for each class period. Students can then report on what they've read, either in class, via a class blog, or in a reading journal. Extensive reading exposes learners to large amounts of input, which facilitates incidental vocabulary learning. If teachers choose to have learners report what they've read on a class blog, learners may link to the material they've found and write a brief response to it or an evaluation of the information.

4

Teaching Listening

Proficiency Guidelines for Listening

As with reading, consult the ACTFL proficiency guidelines for listening at the Advanced and Superior levels (*ACTFL Proficiency Guidelines 2012*).

Research on Listening

Listening can be either interactive or interpretive. Interactive listening occurs in conversations when there are opportunities to ask questions and clarify the meaning of the speaker. The listener and speaker work together to negotiate meaning. The listener actively collaborates using both nonverbal (e.g., nodding, furrowing the brow) and verbal signals (e.g., asking questions or commenting on what was said). Conversely, interpretive listening involves interpretation of meaning in a spoken text where the listener has no opportunity to negotiate or clarify meaning because the creator of the text is absent or not accessible, such as when listening to news broadcasts or lectures. While interactive listening is an important component of language learning, in this volume we will focus on developing interpretive listening skills, as Advanced-level learners are usually quite adept at interactive listening.

Many of the processes involved in reading are also involved in listening, and many of the same factors affect learners' ability to comprehend spoken discourse, including knowledge of the target language, background knowledge, knowledge of how various types of discourses are organized, ability to hold information in short-term memory, and ability to use strategies to construct meaning from the text. Text-based factors, such as length of text, vocabulary, and discourse organization, likewise affect listening comprehension.

Nevertheless, there are several important differences between listening and reading. Written texts, particularly those that are intended for a wide audience, are typically organized into grammatical sentences arranged in coherent paragraphs. Spoken texts, on the other hand, can include ungrammatical or reduced forms; are often marked by pauses, hesitations, and fillers; and may feature topics that shift as the speaker talks. Another difference concerns the "accessibility" of the text (Stevick 1984). Readers can reread texts and can look ahead to predict what is coming. Listeners, on the other hand, may be forced to comprehend with only one opportunity to hear the oral text; lack of attention at any moment may cause the listener to lose part or all of the message. Moreover, readers have control over the pace of the input; they can slow down as necessary. Listeners rarely have that opportunity. Another source of difficulty for listeners is the need to determine word boundaries. In written texts, words and sentences are clearly delineated. In a stream of speech, however, speakers do not pause between words, and listeners may therefore have difficulty "parsing" the information (i.e., deciding where one word begins and another ends).

Scaffolding the Listening Process

Most of the principles associated with teaching reading also apply to teaching listening: (1) activate the learners' prior knowledge in appropriate ways, (2) build vocabulary, (3) teach comprehension, (4) develop strategic listeners, and (5) encourage extensive listening.

As with reading instruction, take care to build the learners' recognition vocabulary. However, remember that learners will not see the new words when they listen to a text. Instead, they must recognize its phonological form in a stretch of speech. Therefore, when preparing for listening texts, it is important that learners hear the new vocabulary rather than just see it. If the word form changes significantly due to morphology, listeners should be made aware of how such a change affects the pronunciation of the word.

Selective Listening

Typically, instructors make use of what Rost (2011) terms "selective listening" in assigned listening/viewing passages. Selective listening involves listening with a planned purpose in mind. This purpose is often to gather specific information related to a task. In other words, selective listening refers to listening only to what you want or need to hear and tuning out everything else. A wide variety of listening tasks can engage students' attention. Following Lund (1990), we suggest several listening tasks or response types that may be appropriate for Advanced- and Superior-level learners:

- *Doing* implies a physical response of some sort.
- *Choosing* involves activities such as putting pictures in order or matching a product to an advertisement.
- *Transferring* might involve drawing, tracing a route, filling in a graph, or other activities in which learners transfer information from one modality to another.
- *Condensing* involves such activities as preparing an outline, completing a graphic organizer, taking notes, or preparing captions for pictures based on the listening passage.
- *Answering* requires completing a set of questions that ask for specific information from the passage.
- *Extending* implies going beyond the text to create an ending, complete a partial transcript, change the text, or embellish it in some way. For debate-based classes, students might be encouraged to think of alternate arguments or make a new closing statement to an opinion piece, or to think of questions to ask the speakers.
- *Modeling* involves imitation of features in the text or of the text as a whole. In a debate class, students could construct an argument based on those heard in the passage.

Pre- and post-listening activities are particularly important for selective listening. Prior to listening, teachers may provide pictures, photos, or cartoons to pique interest in the listening topic and to activate learners' background knowledge. Questions may be used to elicit what students already know about the topic; a KWL chart or anticipated guide may also serve as a pre- and during-listening activity. Effective pre-listening activities heighten the relevance for listening, which in turn motivates learners to listen. Earlier we detailed a number of pre-reading activities, which are also appropriate to prepare learners for listening.

Other Types of Listening

While selective listening is certainly appropriate for language learning, Rost (2011) suggests several other ways of interacting with oral input that may prove useful for teaching various aspects of listening comprehension. Here we list several of Rost's original suggestions.

Intensive Listening

Intensive listening refers to listening closely—for precise sounds, words, phrases, grammatical units, and pragmatic units. Although intensive listening may not be called for in most everyday situations, accurate comprehension is involved in higher level comprehension and listening. The ability to listen intensively *when necessary* is essential for listeners at the Advanced and Superior levels. Listening activities should be designed carefully to facilitate comprehension. The teacher should plan to play a given text multiple times, assigning different tasks with each listening. Earlier tasks should involve the learners in comprehending main ideas. Subsequent tasks should require learners to listen for details or for specific linguistic devices. For instance, learners could be asked to write down three ways in which the speaker signals disagreement.

Dictation, the transcription of the exact words uttered by a speaker, represents a prototypical intensive listening activity. Below are some variations of dictation that make more efficient use of time.

1. *Fast speed dictation.* Read a passage at a natural speed, allowing students to ask for multiple repetitions of any part of the passage but not slowing down the reading of any phrase. This activity is useful for focusing attention on the features of fast speech.
2. *Pause and paraphrase.* Read a passage and pause periodically for students to write paraphrases rather than the exact words heard. This activity focuses students' attention on vocabulary flexibility.
3. *Cloze listening.* Provide a partially completed passage that the students fill in either as they listen or after. This activity allows them to focus on particular language features.

4. *Error identification.* Provide a fully transcribed passage with several errors, either factual or linguistic. The students listen, identify, and correct the errors. This activity focuses on details.
5. *Group dictation.* Learners hear an extended passage, perhaps two minutes long, usually a monologue. The passage should deliberately contain challenging vocabulary and structures, and considerably more information than a single listener can recall after one hearing. Instruct learners *not* to take notes to help build their short-term memory capacity. After the learners have heard the passage once or twice, ask them to collaborate and reconstruct as much of the passage as they can.
6. *Teller and checker.* Students are paired up and assigned roles as either "tellers" or "checkers." After listening to a news story or other text, the teller is assigned to retell the story (or a portion of it) in the target language to the checker, who ensures that the teller is correct and has included all of the relevant details. This technique facilitates collaboration and provides good practice for speaking.
7. *Stop and predict.* At strategic points in the text, stop the audio and ask learners to predict what they will hear next. This technique facilitates development of effective listening strategies.

Responsive Listening

According to Rost (2011, 198), responsive listening "refers to a type of listening in which the listener's response is the goal of the activity. The listener's response in this type of activity is 'affective'—expressing an opinion or point of view—rather than 'informational'—giving back facts based on what was heard." Such an approach is particularly relevant to courses focused on debate. It requires that learners first understand the argument that the speakers are making and then formulate a response. In order for this technique to be effective, teachers must push learners to express themselves using abstract language and extended discourse. A simple "I agree with the speaker" will not promote Superior-level discourse, nor does it demonstrate understanding of the text.

Extensive Listening

As with extensive reading, extensive listening, as described by Willy Renandya and Thomas Farrell (2011, 56) involves "all types of listening activities that allow learners to receive a lot of comprehensible and enjoyable listening input." Assign learners to watch or listen to relevant news stories for each class period. Teachers may allow learners to choose the materials for themselves, abandoning any text that is too difficult at the outset. As with extensive reading, any assessment should be based on completion of the activity alone, rather than on the quality of understanding. Learners may post what they've listened to on a class blog, linking to online sources and commenting on the news source.

Types of Texts

Streaming video of debates is available online in many languages. For listening practice, we recommend directing learners to one or more online debates and having them respond to a set of questions on a handout. In addition, we recommend requiring that learners view at least one hour of programming in the target language on a weekly basis. Such programming need not be limited to debate; rather, we suggest that it reflect participants' personal preferences so that they will look forward to the assignment and, hopefully, want to go above and beyond the required one-hour minimum.

In addition to debates, numerous podcasts are available on a wide variety of topics, many of which are suitable for a debate-based course. Some radio and television stations host programs in which participants discuss controversial topics. Programs similar to *Face the Nation* in the United States are usually at the Superior level and often address current issues that are suitable for in-class debates.

5

Teaching Writing

Proficiency Guidelines for Writing

ACTFL's descriptors of Advanced- and Superior-level writing can provide suggestions for the types of tasks you might assign (*ACTFL Proficiency Guidelines 2012*).

Research on Writing

Writing is an essential component of language proficiency, and it plays an important role in courses on debate. Writing allows learners to express their views on meaningful topics. Moreover, the task of writing a persuasive essay requires a sophisticated level of discourse indicative of the Advanced and Superior levels.

As with L1 writers, students of foreign languages often demonstrate higher oral than written proficiency during the first few years of language instruction. For many, written production never goes beyond "speech-written-down style of writing" (Weissberg 2006, 10). However, in order to reach Superior-level proficiency, a process of "differentiation" between spoken and written language must occur; formal writing makes greater use of syntactic complexity, including more subordinate and embedded clauses, than does oral language (Weissberg 2006). As L2 writers move from Intermediate to Advanced, they are expected to demonstrate ability to connect sentences into paragraphs using cohesive elements and devices (see www.actfl.org for complete descriptors of writing at each level and sublevel). As learners progress toward Superior-level language, their writing should become increasingly sophisticated, demonstrating an ability to connect discourse above the paragraph level, thus further differentiating their written language from their spoken language.

Crafting a sophisticated written argument differs considerably from debating a topic orally; however, the success of the oral debate often depends on the care and attention afforded the former. Learning to write clearly and persuasively requires considerable time and effort for native speakers and L2 learners alike since academic writing reflects a different set of conventions than spoken language, including information gathering, analysis and organization of information, and presentation of ideas in a manner that communicates effectively to the reader (Williams 2005).

Robert Kaplan (1987) observes that oral and written argumentation are similar in that they aim to persuade the audience. As with speaking, supporting and defending opinions and constructing hypotheses and conjectures are core tasks at the Superior level. Moreover, language users at this level must be able to write in a variety of content areas, including practical, professional, and social topics, and must be able to form cohesive text of multiple paragraphs and pages, and demonstrate good control of grammatical structures and a sophisticated range of vocabulary. Accuracy, cultivated in the reflective skill of writing, contributes not only to improved written proficiency but to overall improved oral proficiency (Brown, Bown, and Eggett 2009; Brecht, Davidson, and Ginsberg 1995; Higgs and Clifford 1982; Magnan and Back 2007).

Genres

Certain genres of writing correspond with particular proficiency levels. For Advanced-level learners, travel logs, news stories, personal narratives, and descriptions are appropriate genres. The purpose of Advanced-level writers is to inform, and their texts are typically of a factual nature. Superior-level writers, on the other hand, are expected to persuade. Genres appropriate for Superior-level writers include editorials, critical responses to others' writing, synthesis and analysis of research, and policy papers and reports of an academic nature. Keeping the genres in mind will ensure that instruction is targeted to the correct level of proficiency. If writers have not yet attained Advanced Mid in their writing proficiency, provide plenty of practice with Advanced-level tasks before asking learners to produce Superior-level writing. Summaries of factual papers or informational reports related to a controversial topic should precede the writing of persuasive or analytical essays.

Genre Analysis

Teachers should consider genres not only when assigning tasks but also when preparing learners to write in a given genre. Research shows that genre conventions vary from culture to culture (Zhu 2005). Thus, an important component of teaching writing is to introduce learners to the conventions associated with a chosen genre, including structure, lexicon, syntactic features, and so on. As learners become familiar with genres, their written expression improves not only in terms of accuracy and complexity but also in terms of cultural appropriateness.

Teachers should seek out authentic models and then guide learners through the process of genre analysis. Multiple models addressed to different audiences can help learners develop an awareness of register. Teachers can prepare questions to that effect, and that draw attention to specific parts of the text that signal the introduction, thesis, and so on. Sample questions or tasks include the following: (1) Which lines of the passage represent the introduction? (2) Find an example of a definition, and (3) Where is the author's thesis? Learners also may be asked to assess the organization of the passage, perhaps by using a graphic organizer or by outlining what they have read.

After broader questions, the learners might be asked to pay attention to specific linguistic features of the text, including use of passive voice or verb tenses that may differ from what they are used to seeing. For example, an English-language class for advanced writers might focus on writing a research paper. In the methods section, the teacher might draw their attention to the use of "left-dislocation" to express purpose (i.e., in English, moving the "purpose" statement to the beginning of the sentence: "In order to assess the validity of X, researchers also employed. . . .").

Following a close analysis of at least one textual model, learners may then construct a text with the class and teacher as a whole. This can be accomplished effectively using Google docs or a Wiki, where multiple individuals are able to edit a document at the same time and to see the changes that others are making. Once the students have collaborated on a document, the teacher may then guide them through such tasks as combining sentences, addressing inadequacies in organization, and suggesting more appropriate words.

Teachers may also guide learners through the process of writing a thesis statement, drafting introductions and conclusions, and writing paragraphs. In the *Mastering Languages through Global Debate* series, learners not only read samples of good thesis statements, they also closely examine and evaluate samples of poor thesis statements and discuss how they can be improved. Similarly, they evaluate introductions and conclusions. You may ask students to fix a poor example after explaining the problems.

Teaching Writing

As with teaching any foreign language skill, attention must be given to scaffolding the writing process. Learners need guidance through pre-writing, writing, and post-writing phases to help them generate ideas, formulate them appropriately in the target language, and complete the task. Moreover, learners may need focused practice on syntax to help them improve the complexity of their writing.

Designing the Writing Task

An important first step in teaching writing is designing an appropriate writing task. This involves not only choosing a task appropriate to the learners' proficiency (see the sample writing assignment, following) but also presenting the task to learners clearly. Too often teachers give learners little or no explanation as to the assignment itself. A typical writing assignment might read, "Write a five hundred–word essay about environmental protection versus economic growth." However, such an assignment fails to explain the purpose of the assignment and the audience, information that will help the learner better fulfill the task. When creating a writing assignment, make certain to answer the following questions for yourself and then communicate those answers to your students. The following is a writing assignment that addresses all of these issues.

Sample Writing Assignment

Topic: Environmental protection vs. economic growth

Purpose: Your purpose in writing this essay is to take a stand for either environmental protection or economic growth, to challenge your reader to evaluate his own position, and to persuade your reader to agree with your position.

Audience: Your audience for this paper will be the university students in Russia with whom you will be debating the issue. Assume that your reader holds the opposing position.

Style: Though your audience is made up of students, your tone should still be formal and academic. A paper that is written in a very colloquial style will make you sound less credible.

Format: The paper should be 3–5 pages in length, double-spaced, with 1-inch margins and 12-point font. Use the *Chicago Manual of Style* for documenting your sources.

Content: Your paper must have the following components:

Introduction: The introduction should include a clear thesis statement. Introduce the topic and orient the reader to the ways in which you will develop the topic. Include a definition of environmental protection or economic development. The thesis statement is a direct, explicit assertion explaining your position and the arguments that you will make.

Body: You will develop arguments in support of your position by providing expert opinion, findings from academic studies, case examples, and facts and theories based on the sources that you find. Develop each supporting argument clearly and in detail, using source material directly and explicitly to support your position. You must document your sources in the body of the text using parenthetical documentation and in a Works Cited page. Remember that you must challenge and overcome your reader's strong biases and must address and disprove the strongest argument in support of the opposing view.

Conclusion: Your conclusion should include a summary of the main arguments that you have made in the paper, but it should also demonstrate the significance of your arguments.

WHAT IS THE PURPOSE OF THE ASSIGNMENT?

If students are writing position papers, their purpose is to persuade their audience that their position is correct. In order to do so, they must also be prepared to cite evidence in support of their positions and to explain the relevance of the evidence. However, you may assign different types of papers. Perhaps you want students to analyze a situation, explaining, for instance, what global warming is, what its likely causes are, and what the future effects may be. Or perhaps you wish for them to write a policy paper, detailing the actions that a particular organization should take to ensure security. Whatever the purpose is, make sure to clearly explain it to the learners.

WHO IS THE AUDIENCE?

Often we assume that the instructor—or the person grading the paper—is the only audience. However, it is useful to think of a broader audience. If students are writing a position paper, they may be directed to write to the readers of a particular newspaper (as part of an editorial) or to a group of students in their target community.

WHAT STYLE IS APPROPRIATE?

Do you expect the students to choose a more formal, scholarly style, or would a personal style (using first person) be more appropriate for this assignment?

WHAT FORMAT IS EXPECTED FOR THE ASSIGNMENT?

Instead of simply giving learners a page limit, clarify requirements for font sizes, margins, line spacing, and headings. Moreover, consider documentation. Will students be required to cite outside resources? If so, which style guide is preferred?

Using Detailed Assignment Instructions and Grading Rubrics

Once you have designed the assignment, consider providing a handout explaining the assignment in more detail, including specific guidance on purpose, content, audience, style, format, and any other important aspects of the paper.

Giving students a scoring guide or grading rubric that lists the criteria that will be used to evaluate their writing is also a good idea. If students know from the outset what their teacher is looking for in a paper, they will be able to put their energy into meeting these expectations. (Earlier we provided an example of detailed instructions for a position paper, and appendix B includes an example of a grading rubric used to evaluate students' papers.)

Suggestions for Writing Assignments

In order to give students substantial writing practice, we recommend a variety of writing assignments that focus on different aspects of writing. In addition, we recommend that teachers not only focus on activities for "learning to write" but also for "writing to learn." Learning to write activities are those tasks designed primarily to foster the development of writing skills. Writing to learn activities, on the other hand, recognize that writing fosters critical thinking. Such activities are typically short, impromptu, or otherwise informal assignments designed to help learners think through key concepts discussed in the course. Writing to learn assignments can help students prepare for class discussions and, ultimately, for longer writing assignments.

WRITING TO LEARN ACTIVITIES

In this section we highlight several writing to learn activities that might be useful in a debate-oriented course, including reading journals, reader response charts, and dialogue journals.

Reading Journals

Reading journals can be helpful for recording observations and questions. If reading a persuasive essay, learners can write their initial responses to the piece. Instructors may also wish to provide more specific questions to guide students' thinking, such as:

- What did you understand least in today's assignment?
- What points in the article that you read for today are most (or least) convincing? Why?
- What assumptions do you make about the author of this piece based on what you read?

Reading journals can be used for assigned readings, or may be used in conjunction with an extensive reading program, in which learners are directed to find articles on their own, read them, and respond to them. Reading journals help learners to engage more deeply with the text and make them more conscious of the role the reader plays in "meaning making." They also can be used to foster discussion in class, particularly if all learners have read the same text. Instructors may assign the journals to be written outside of class or give five minutes at the beginning of class to respond to the questions. In class, learners may be directed to swap journals with another student, who then must respond to what his or her peer has written.

Reader Response Charts

Sometimes students need to be reminded that they bring their own biases to the topics about which they are reading and that these biases affect their receptivity to the texts. One activity designed to facilitate self-reflection involves using a reader response chart. Learners make two columns on a sheet of paper, one titled, "The author's prejudices," and the second titled, "My prejudices." Identifying the biases of the author facilitates critical reading, and noting their own prejudices can also help them to better understand their responses to the text. Reader response charts can be used to foster in-class discussions. Moreover, during class, teachers may direct learners to find linguistic devices used to signal the author's bias. Such a close reading of the text will improve students' awareness of text construction.

Dialogue Journals/Letters

Particularly as learners are formulating their arguments for oral and written debate, they can benefit from written dialogue with other classmates or, ideally, with native speakers. Via online forums, blogs, or physical texts (either handwritten or typed), learners may write their initial opinions on the assigned topic. They then exchange their opinion with another student who must respond in writing.

Asynchronous Online Writing Activities

The internet offers learners a public forum for retrieving information, sharing ideas, and publishing the product of their work. Publicly presenting ideas provides learners with a real audience and purpose beyond the simple fulfilling of an assignment. Online writing tools include Web forums, wikis, and blogs.

Web Forums

Many online learning systems, such as Blackboard and Moodle, include features like class discussion boards. In this closed format, the instructor may post questions for the students to answer, or students may be assigned to write a post that generates a discussion. Some instructors may decide to periodically meet "virtually." Doing so will allow learners to discuss a topic in writing, thus forcing them to pay more attention to the language that they are using.

Wikis

Wikis are collaborative websites that reflect the collective work of many people. They allow anyone (or anyone who is authorized) to add, delete, or edit the content posted on a given site. Wikis allow students to build on each other's knowledge as they collaborate on texts, thus facilitating social constructivist learning. As they create wikis, students learn to communicate ideas effectively and to build consensus with their colleagues. In debate-oriented classes, wikis may be used to document evidence for or against a particular topic. For example, in a discussion of affirmative action, learners may create a Wiki documenting evidence that affirmative action has increased the number of minorities who graduate from college.

Blogs

Blogs are an increasingly popular way to engage learners in authentic writing. Blogs are meant to be read and commented on, thus allowing learners to serve as coproducers. Blogging provides learners additional opportunities to debate issues under consideration. The methodical nature of writing facilitates increased reflection, and the public posting of discussions contributes to an understanding of the opposing side, clarification of opinions, and opportunities to comment on students' arguments as well as on their language use.

Blogs can be used within a single class or they can be shared with a partner institution in the target language culture. Students may blog at any point during the process. For example, they may blog before the formal debates as a means of clarifying their thinking and gathering ideas. Similarly, students may blog following a formal debate to offer additional arguments or further clarifications of their opinions, or simply as a means of reflecting on the debate itself.

Student blogging can present some challenges to the teacher, including, as Mark Sample (2012) noted in the *Humanities and Technology Camp* blog, the structure of the blog, the rhythm of postings, and finally the roles played by students. Sample lists two possible structures for the classroom blog: the hub-and-spoke approach and the centralized class blog. In the hub-and-spoke model, each student creates his or her own blog, and the teacher aggregates their postings on the main blog. Centralized classroom blogs provide all learners' accounts on one blog, where they all post and make comments.

The rhythm of postings can vary from the free-for-all model in which learners must post ten (or some other number of blogs) during the semester. A variation on this is to stipulate that no more than three blogs can be posted during any given week to prevent students from writing all of their assignments at the end of the semester. In the checkpoint model, learners must submit a certain number of blogs by particular checkpoints throughout the semester. There is also the assigned deadline method, in which all students (or certain subsets of students) must post by a given date, or perhaps weekly.

Finally, consider the roles played by students in the classroom blog. Sample suggests assigning roles so that not every student is posting at the same time. Moreover, students can be given separate tasks each week. Among the task assignments recommended by Sample are that of (1) first readers: those who are responsible for generating the discussion by posting initial questions and insights about the topic to the blog the day before the class meets; (2) respondents: those who respond to the first readers by the next class meeting; and (3) searchers: those who find and share at least one relevant online resource. In addition to posting the link to the resource, learners must provide a short evaluation of the resource, noting what makes it worthwhile, unusual, or even problematic.

ASSESSING WRITING TO LEARN ACTIVITIES
Writing to learn activities are meant to be informal. Teachers may choose to assign points for completion—perhaps learners must complete at least ten reading journals or five dialogue journals during the semester. Another option is to ask students to select a certain number of their best assignments to be scored holistically, focusing on the content and the development of ideas rather than on the language. Students may choose the best assignments in collaboration with peers.

LEARNING TO WRITE ACTIVITIES
In this section we detail a variety of activities ranging in length from paragraphs to full essays and varying in focus from those focused primarily on form to exercises focused primarily on meaning. Among the activities detailed here are rapid writings, sentence outlines, summaries, renderings, paraphrases, sentence-combining activities, extending sentences, and position papers. Note that rapid writings, outlines, and summaries can also be viewed or used as "writing to learn" activities. Writing of summaries and outlines (if learners are outlining a text they have read or heard) can help learners to better process the information in the text and lead to deeper understanding.

Rapid Writings
Rapid writings are timed writing exercises in which learners are asked to write extemporaneously on a target language topic. These exercises can be used for assessment, for "writing to learn," and for improvement of fluency in writing.

By way of assessment, rapid writings can help teachers gauge the initial proficiency level of learners. At the beginning of a semester, teachers may give students twenty minutes to take a stand on a particular issue (e.g., American automobiles are a better value than European, or professional athletes are paid excessively). Students are directed to write for twenty minutes without access to dictionaries or online translators. When the time limit is up, students must stop writing. The writing samples procured by this method will help teachers to know what their students' strengths and weaknesses are in order to design appropriate writing tasks and to place students into appropriate peer review groups.

Rapid writing assignments may be used as "writing to learn" activities during the semester. At the beginning of a new unit, by way of introduction to the topic, teachers may assign learners to write for a specified amount of time (perhaps no more than five) on the topic. Giving a similar assignment midway through each unit not only allows additional extemporaneous writing practice but also helps learners use the vocabulary and structures they've learned. Moreover, if the students have preserved their initial writing sample, they can compare their progress.

Sentence Outlines

After students read assigned texts for a given topic, or before they write a full essay, consider asking students to write a sentence outline in the target language. Writing a sentence outline helps learners formulate their thoughts and articulate them in an abbreviated format. A sentence outline comprises all of the components of a full-length persuasive essay, the one main distinction being that it distills one's ideas down to essential claims and supporting evidence without any attempt made at elaborating ideas or transitioning between main body paragraphs. The basic components are as follows: thesis statement, counterargument (optional), argument 1, evidence 1, argument 2, evidence 2, argument 3, evidence 3, and conclusion.

Summaries

The ability to write summaries of an article is an Advanced-level language skill that can help learners prepare for Superior-level tasks. Students may write summaries of texts that they have read or heard. This allows learners both to distill the information to the essential components and to develop transitions. Summarizing requires a close reading of the text, the distillation of the ideas contained in it, and a reformulation of the ideas in the writer's own words. A good summary should

- contain a clear topic sentence, expressing the main idea(s) of the original author or the main findings based on a set of data;
- include major supporting ideas and arguments;
- state the source;
- use different language than the original text; and
- be shorter than the original text.

Teachers may wish to assign a sentence outline of an assigned text prior to a summary to scaffold the writing process. Once students have completed a sentence outline, they can then use connectors and more complex structures to produce connected discourse.

Renderings

Students may be asked to read a text in their native language and then to write a target language version of the paper. Rendering is similar to writing a summary except that the writer is asked to work with a text in his or her native language and then summarize it in the target language. It differs from translation in its goal, which is to write a summary of the main ideas. The task is more complex than summarizing because the writer must have a better grasp of the necessary vocabulary to effectively render the text. As a follow-up, teachers may ask learners to compare their renderings with those of classmates or native speakers. As learners compare their own writing to that of native speakers, they are able to "notice the gap" (Schmidt and Frota 1986, 310) or become aware of the differences between their own language production and that of native speakers.

Sentence Combining / Reformulation

Thomas Cooper (1981) demonstrated that guiding students through sentence-combining activities improved the syntactic complexity of their writing. Similarly, Schultz (1994) suggests that learners engage in reformulation activities in which they (1) analyze a poorly written text consisting of only three or four sentences, (2) revise the text, and (3) compare their rewritten version to one that has been rewritten by a native speaker. Learners can benefit from both good models and poor examples if they are given an opportunity to analyze weaknesses and improve on them. For a more holistic writing activity, learners may also be asked to identify gaps in the reasoning and arguments of the paper and then to strengthen the paper by including support for assertions, and so on.

Paraphrasing

For writers at the Advanced level, paraphrasing represents an effective means of building their vocabulary and expanding their syntactical repertoire. Teachers provide learners with short texts that should then be rewritten using different sentence structures and vocabulary. Instructors may wish to have learners focus on a particular paraphrasing skill each time, such as using synonyms, changing the voice from passive to active, changing nouns to verbs, combining sentences with conjunctions, using subordination to combine sentences, and so on.

Position Papers

Position papers serve as the culminating writing exercise for the debate course. We recommend that position papers extend to two typed pages and articulate clearly and persuasively a student's assigned position (i.e., for or against a given issue). Instructors may choose to allow learners to argue their own feelings or, as we recommend, they may assign positions to the learners. Almost invariably, students will find themselves, at least on one occasion, having to defend a position with which they do not agree in the first place. Doing so enhances their critical thinking skills and pushes them to articulate a coherent argument—and in a foreign language no less.

Teachers may choose to assign position papers at the end of each unit, or to help learners build up to position papers by assigning smaller writing tasks throughout the course. The advantage of the former approach is that the writing and preparation for the oral debate go hand in hand. The second approach affords more opportunities for learners to write at the Superior level by building on the level of sophistication required for each writing assignment. Regardless of the approach, we recommend that teachers walk learners through the writing process step by step. The approach used in *Mastering English through Global Debate* includes a specific focus on writing at the end of each unit. Initially learners are directed to good sources of information to research their topic. Next they practice developing a thesis statement. As part of this process students read examples of effective thesis statements. They also evaluate a variety of thesis statements to determine which are most effective and work together to fix less effective sentences. Learners are then expected to draft a thesis statement and bring it to class for evaluation and comment.

After drafting the thesis statement, learners develop a sentence outline that includes their thesis statement as well as their arguments, along with evidence in support of their arguments. Students may first outline sample position papers to gain an understanding of the structure(s) of such a paper.

After they develop the outline, it's time for students to turn their sentences into paragraphs. As with preparation to write a thesis statement, students are first given a chance to analyze and evaluate paragraphs. In particular, they check to ensure that the paragraph has a single unifying idea with an identifiable topic statement. Students revise paragraphs that either have extraneous information or weak topic sentences before writing the body of their position papers.

The next step is developing the introduction and conclusion. To help learners write effective introductions and conclusions, it is useful to have them read several effective examples and to note the devices used to grab the reader's attention. After analyzing and editing introductions and conclusions, learners write their own and add them to their papers.

Before students submit their position papers, they should be taught to read their own work critically and to revise as necessary. Learners frequently skip or minimize this process, often printing (or emailing) their finished papers before they've read over them at all. When student writers do read over their own work, it's often merely to fix sentence-level errors rather than to think about the paper as a whole. Teachers can facilitate the revision process by having students work through it in class. Learners may first be directed to highlight their thesis statement and the topic sentence of each paragraph. They should then read through the highlighted statements twice. When reviewing the highlighted statements the first time, readers should critically evaluate whether each topic sentence aligns with the paper's thesis. If not, learners should rewrite the sentences or the thesis statement, or eliminate a topic sentence (and paragraph) altogether. The second time learners read through their sentences, they should pay attention to the organization of the paper, asking themselves whether the order of the topic sentences is logical. Finally, learners should read the whole paper, not just the key sentences, focusing on each paragraph. They should make sure that each paragraph has a clear idea and the topic sentence adequately expresses the main idea. This same process can also be used for peer reviews of written work or in writing conferences with students.

Preparing Learners to Write

Designing the writing assignment is just the first step in guiding learners through the writing process. Once students understand the assignment and the grading criteria, they will be better prepared to think about the topic that they will address. However, choosing a topic and generating ideas can be difficult. Virginia Scott (1992, cited in Shrum and Glisan 2010) suggests that generating ideas is the most challenging feature of the foreign language writing process because learners tend to use L1 idea-generation strategies and only later transfer or translate these ideas to their L2. Silva (1993) also contends that L2 writers spend less time planning and organizing their ideas than do L1 writers and, as a result, have great difficulty with these steps. Thus, in teaching writing, it is particularly important to guide learners through a pre-writing process to help them generate ideas and begin planning for their paper. Below are some methods that can be used in class to help students come up with ideas for their papers.

Listing

Lead a discussion in which students call out possible ideas or topics for the assignment while you write them down for everyone to see. At this stage do not rule out any ideas; simply let one idea lead to another. After five or ten minutes of listing, have students write down ideas for their own papers. Following is a list of topics generated by students for the position paper assignment referred to earlier.

Sample Brainstorming Results

Environmental Protection vs. Economic Growth

Oil spill in the Gulf of Mexico cost billions in lost business
Chemical leaks into water supplies
Lack of potable water in some areas
Kyoto protocols
Increased health problems from air pollution
Dangers of cutting down the rain forests
Benefits of rain forests
Dwindling shelter for animals forces more wild animals into residential areas

Freewriting

Freewriting is a way for learners to generate ideas without worrying about form and accuracy. It encourages students to begin the writing process, overcoming any mental or emotional blocks that they may be facing. Moreover, the ideas generated during freewriting can help learners focus their thoughts. Set a timer for five to ten minutes and direct learners to write everything they can think of in connection with the assignment. Learners may choose to write in complete sentences or in bullet points. They also need not worry about spelling or grammar. Most students will be surprised to find that their ideas are already forming.

Clustering

The goal of clustering (also known as webbing or mapping) is to help students move from a more general idea to a more focused topic for a paper. Additionally, it may serve as an initial structure for a paper. Either as a whole class or individually, list the main idea for a paper in a circle in the middle of a page or on the blackboard. Draw lines out from the center to various possible subheadings, and then additional lines from the subheadings to the next possible level (see figure 2 for an example).

Talking

Students often find that their ideas begin to flow when they talk with others about their topic. Teachers may try some form of "pair shares," in which the students choose partners to talk with. Some variations involve "think pair shares," in which students are given a minute to think about what they would like to say, or "jot pair shares" in which they jot down their ideas first before choosing a partner with whom to talk. It can be helpful to designate one partner as the "listener" and the other as the "talker" for a set period of time. The listener should ask good questions and provide encouragement. The students will then switch roles. After the talking exercise, have learners write down the ideas they came up with as they talked.

Invention

After generating ideas, learners must begin the process of formulating those ideas in the target language in appropriate ways. As part of the invention stage, consider teaching learners to use available linguistic resources, such as dictionaries, both bilingual and monolingual; online translators; and online language corpora. (See table 2 for sample corpus-based exercises taken from *Mastering English through Global Debate*.) Research suggests that learners often lack understanding about how to use such resources

Figure 2: Environment Cluster Exercise

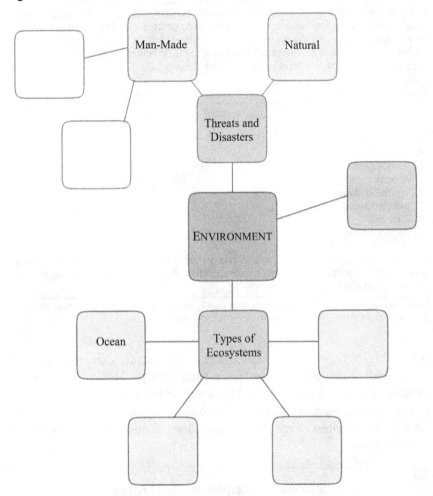

Note: To download a PDF of the illustrations in this book, please visit http://press.georgetown.edu/book/languages/teaching-advanced-language-skills-through-global-debate.

appropriately and training in "invention" strategies—that is, finding appropriate lexical items, collocations, and grammatical structures.

Drafting

Once learners understand the genre in which they must write and the requirements of the assignment, and once they have generated ideas, it is

Table 2. Corpus-Based Exercise

A. Go to the Corpus of Contemporary American English (COCA) (http://corpus.byu.edu/coca/) and find three collocates commonly used in conjunction with the following words. To do this, type the word in the words box and then type "[v*]" in the collocates box. Under "Sorting and Limits" find the dropdown menu next to the "Minimum" and select "Mutual Info." Type each collocate in the Word(s) box and click Search.

Foreign and Domestic Affairs	Corresponding Collocates		
1. Resolution	1. adopt	2. pass	3. authorize
2. Coalition			
3. Intervention			
4. Genocide			
5. Democracy			
6. Atrocities			
7. Territorial Integrity			
8. Independence			
9. Civil War			
10. Armed Forces			

B. Choose five words concerning foreign and domestic affairs from the table in A. Write a sentence for each word and one of its corresponding collocates that describe foreign and/or domestic affairs in your home country.

Note: To download a PDF of the illustrations in this book, please visit http://press.georgetown.edu/book/languages/teaching-advanced-language-skills-through-global-debate.

time to begin the writing process. In the drafting stage, learners write their initial draft, either on their own or in small groups. This process may be broken down into smaller steps. Although "revising" is listed as a separate step in the following, it should also be considered part of the drafting process. Before learners share their writing, they should be taught to revise their own work.

Sharing and Responding to Writing

Upon completing a rough draft, students assess their own work and then review each other's work during class. The peer review process reinforces in the writers' minds the criteria by which their work will be rated and, more importantly, informs them of the areas that need improvement. To facilitate the peer review process, learners must receive some training or guidance in responding to written language. For example, instruct learners to focus their peer review comments primarily on content, with secondary attention given to form. In so doing, the peer-reviewing process contributes to students' understanding of what constitutes a substantive and well-organized paper, regardless of the language in which it is written. Given that the primary emphasis of the task relates to content rather than form, encourage learners without requiring that they comment in the target language on each other's written compositions. In addition, consider providing learners with a list of questions for them to consider as they read their classmates' written work. (See following sample questions.)

Sample Peer Review Questions

1. Does the opening paragraph grab your attention?
2. Is there a thesis? If so, what is it? How might the thesis be improved?
3. Are the ideas supported with enough examples (both paraphrases and quotations)?
4. Examine the structure of the essay. Does it hang together well? Can readers follow easily? Are there any jarring transitions? If so, where? Are there any particularly smooth transitions?
5. Overall, are words, phrases, and sentences clear? Give an example of a particularly clear sentence. Give an example of a sentence that could be clearer.
6. Is the textual proof cited properly?
7. Is the conclusion effective? Does it avoid adding new information?
8. Overall, what are some of the strengths of the paper?
9. What areas do you think the person should work on when revising?

If circumstances allow, consider organizing consultations with native speakers who have been trained to provide feedback on writing and to help learners write with more sophisticated language. Train consultants to focus not only on grammar but also on issues of content and organization as well as on the writer's potential audience. The consultants can help learners recognize colloquialisms and provide more native-like models. When dealing with errors, consultants should not simply correct a student's mistakes but should point out a problem and elicit ideas from the author as to what could be problematic with the construction and how to correct it. This approach engages students in the revision process and emphasizes ownership of the final version.

Revising

In this stage, learners act on the feedback that they have received either from peers or from the instructor to improve their writing. This stage should involve fixing global problems rather than local problems.

Editing

Once the major revisions are made, learners should begin to polish their essays, checking for surface-level errors in spelling, punctuation, and grammar.

Students then revise and resubmit their assignments, taking into account feedback from both the peer reviewer and native speaker assistant. Consider requiring that learners submit revisions using "track changes" or bold-faced characters to distinguish revised text from the original. Alternatively, if students have used Wikis or Google Docs, access previous versions to note changes from one version to another.

Publishing

Publishing means "making public." This may involve little more than turning in the final written product for a grade. However, many students find it motivating to share their work with a wider audience. The internet makes publishing possible: learners may publish their work on a class discussion site, via a class Wiki, or on a personal blog. Other options for publishing include sending the work to native speakers for response or possibly sharing the written work orally in the form of a presentation.

Feedback and Correction

When providing feedback and correction, instructors have a number of rubrics to choose from. There really is no one right or wrong approach; the key is to be consistent. In this volume, we include a rubric that reflects a synthesis of criteria from the ACTFL Oral Proficiency Interview, Written Proficiency Test Rating Grid, and the Presentational Mode Rubric (Adair-Hauck, Glisan, and Troyan 2013). The rubric incorporates both global outcomes and fine-grained criteria, including content, vocabulary, grammar, and impact (see appendix B). The rubric specifies three main proficiency levels that correspond with ACTFL levels: Fair (10–13 points) corresponds with Intermediate High; Good (14–15 points) corresponds with Advanced Mid; Very Good (16–17 points) means that learners are approaching Superior; and Excellent (18–20 points) reflects Superior.

6

Teaching Speaking

Speaking Proficiency Guidelines

For a detailed description of the ACTFL speaking proficiency guidelines, refer to "Overview of Proficiency Guidelines" in this volume, or review ACTFL's descriptors of Advanced- and Superior-level speaking (*ACTFL Proficiency Guidelines 2012*).

Research on Speaking

In discussing the function of rhetoric, Edward Inch and Barbara Warnick (2005, 114) assert that "the rhetorical function of language aims to direct or influence thoughts and behavior. It is persuasive." Additional research, including that conducted by J. Massie (2005) and Ulla Connor (1987), identifies the task of argumentation and debate as a valuable strategy in improving L2 oral and written proficiency, especially at the Advanced and Superior levels. The task of supporting and defending opinions is a core task at the Superior level, and the criteria outlined in the ACTFL speaking performance profile dovetail precisely with qualities emphasized in public speaking and debate.

1. *Pronunciation.* Linguists and orators of world languages have produced a vast body of literature that addresses challenges unique to pronunciation in specific languages. Such efforts aimed at codifying

a standard pronunciation often end up ostracizing individuals whose pronunciation differs from the established norm, similar to how speakers of a "low" language in a diglossic speech community become ostracized from speakers of the "high" language. As Ferguson (1959, 330) points out, even where such prejudices do not exist, there remains an underlying belief that the high language is "somehow more beautiful, more logical, better able to express important thoughts, and the like."[11] While Superior-level pronunciation may not always qualify as that of an educated native speaker, it certainly approximates it to the point where native speakers rarely become disturbed by it.

2. *Fluency/integrative abilities.* In terms of fluency of speech, the Superior-level speaker easily connects extended thoughts, thus moving beyond sentential-level speech to that of connected, cohesive paragraphs. Fluency of speech likewise characterizes an experienced public speaker, particularly in societies that have a high regard for interpersonal communication skills.

3. *Vocabulary.* Superior-level speakers can participate in a wide variety of conversations, ranging from professional or scholarly to informal topics, and can tailor their language accordingly. Although circumlocution represents a valuable skill developed by Superior-level speakers in order to engage individuals on an array of topics, frequent usage of a relatively limited number of vocabulary items often results in "inexpressive and boring speech" (Fessenden et al. 1973, 92). Redding (1954, 205) further asserts that "although it should be obvious that argumentative discourse requires extraordinary precision in vocabulary, many debaters have been known to toss about, with gleeful abandon, vague and ambiguous terms. The debater, like any public speaker, should command a precision of word choice that will reflect the most subtle shadings of meaning." In short, breadth of vocabulary facilitates fluency and accuracy and expands a debater's capacity to provide uninterrupted, extended, in-depth discourse on a topic, rather than spotty, fragmented statements that lack transitions, cohesion, and continuity.

4. *Sociolinguistic/cultural appropriateness.* Debate challenges an individual's ability to demonstrate intellectual prowess, cultural sophistication, and wittiness. Superior-level speakers distinguish themselves in their ability to make cultural references to the target language culture, employ idiomatic statements, and control the range of registers needed

to respond appropriately in professional situations and in conversational settings using colloquial language. As Philipsen (1992, 12) observed, "Speaking is always speaking somewhere, with some group of people, in some language, and it is always shaped by and a part of some social life. To understand speaking in a particular instance is, in part, to understand a distinctive way of life." Massie (2005) likewise emphasizes the importance of memorizing a critical mass of cultural background information, particularly at the Superior level and higher.

5. *Grammatical accuracy.* Correct usage of grammar naturally plays an important role in any public speaking forum. Sentence construction in oral presentation tends to have a looser structure than in most forms of writing, but certainly not at the expense of grammatical rules. Similarly, a Superior-level speaker may make occasional grammatical errors, but one does not notice a recurring pattern of errors, especially with regard to basic structures.

6. *Tasks.* Debate topics can be understood in terms of a set of basic questions, also referred to as stasis questions (i.e., questions of conjecture, definition, cause and consequence, value, and procedure and proposal; see "Types of Arguments," below). Depending on the issue, certain types of questions will be more applicable than others.

Types of Arguments

Like a game of chess, there are different strategies that can be used in debate. The Greek philosophers suggested at least five points of stasis, or the imaginary points in the mind of the audience where arguments *for* clash with arguments *against.* They are listed below in the form of questions that could be used as part of a debate strategy.

1. *Conjecture (What if . . . ?) questions.* What would happen if we gave top priority to economic development all the time in all situations? When making a conjecture argument, we propose a hypothetical, or "what if, then," statement that is a positive logical extension of your position, or a negative logical extension of the other side.

2. *Definition questions.* What does *environment* mean? Are humans as much a part of the environment as animals and the weather? Definition arguments entail clearly understanding and defining the words, phrases, and arguments that can be used to support or reject an idea. The starting point for this strategy is dictionary definitions. However, phrases, words, and ideas can also be defined.

3. *Cause and consequence questions.* What are the likely results of an increase in global temperatures? Cause and consequence (or cause and effect) arguments address the relationship between something happening and what occurs as a result.

4. *Value questions.* Do human beings have a responsibility to protect the environment, such as the Brazilian rainforest, even at the expense of improving human life? Value questions ask whether something is good or bad, beautiful or ugly, better or worse. We examine, agree with, or challenge the qualities of an idea. Consider, for example, the topic of immigration. Those who approach this issue from a values perspective typically develop a set of criteria or points that support the value in question. For example, "Immigration is good because it leads to X, Y, and Z happening, which, everyone can agree, are good things."

5. *Procedural questions.* How do we develop an approach to sustainability that both protects the environment as well as helps nations develop economically? Procedural questions focus on the future by extending an argument into a future reality and questioning how feasible, plausible, or credible that future may be. Say the topic under debate addresses the balance between security and freedom. Most discussions that use a procedural argument will talk about what kind of world we will have if we have too much security, too little freedom, or the alternatives. For example, one side could describe what living in a nation would be like if security were seen as more important than personal freedom.

Determining Positions

At the start of a new topic, create new teams for the proposition and opposition. This can be accomplished in a number of ways. Some factors to consider in creating teams include the proficiency range of participants and how to give students of varying abilities a chance to work together on teams, odd or even numbers of students and whether or not to account for a rotating alternate, gender distribution across teams, and the like. Developing an algorithm of sorts to account for multiple variables can become a tedious and time-consuming task. A considerably simpler yet surprisingly effective approach entails assigning each position a letter (e.g., Team A equals the proposition and Team B the opposition), and having participants draw a letter. The letter a participant draws determines the position he or she will adopt and the team he or she will join for a given chapter.

Regardless of the approach to creating heterogeneous teams whose members hold differing views, exposing learners to diverse perspectives on an issue facilitates cognitive growth and encourages open-mindedness. Learners should be instructed to clearly articulate their own positions and to listen carefully and respectfully to the viewpoints of fellow students.

Corners

Students move to one corner of the room based on their stance on a particular issue. For instance, students may move to a corner of the room that represents their level of agreement with a particular statement (strongly agree, agree, disagree, strongly disagree). If the learners are equally distributed, consider forming four-member teams by taking a pair of students from two different sides of the room (i.e., students espousing different positions). Within these four-member teams, have students who share the same viewpoint discuss their best arguments. After a designated period of time, reconstitute the four-member team and have the pairs share their ideas with one another. At the conclusion of this procedure, have all four students work together to create a final product that represents the best arguments for both sides of the issue.

Value Line

On opposite sides of the room, post signs that read: "strongly agree" and "strongly disagree." Put a line of masking tape down the middle of the room connecting the two signs. Then orally or in writing present a controversial statement, such as, "Government has the right to spy on its citizens in order to protect them from terrorist acts." Give students a few minutes to write down their answers along with one argument to support their viewpoint. Next ask participants to "take a stand" by positioning themselves along the tape between "strongly agree" and "strongly disagree." This line serves as an opinion spectrum. From this rank-ordered line, form teams of four (or more) people, by joining someone from each end of the continuum as well as two learners standing nearer the middle.

Scaffolding the Speaking Process

As with other L2 modalities, students must be adequately prepared for oral communication. In addition to familiarizing themselves with the necessary vocabulary, students need opportunities to generate ideas, research content, and otherwise plan how they will carry out oral tasks. Reading texts related to the topic and listening to oral commentary will help familiarize learners with the issues at hand and the variety of perspectives that are available. Such activities have the added benefit of building learners' reading and listening comprehension skills.

In addition to reading and listening, give learners time to adequately brainstorm. Brainstorming can be done in pairs or as a class led by the teacher. In addition to generating ideas for debate and discussion, consider asking students to brainstorm the kinds of language, both vocabulary and grammatical structures, that they might need to complete the task. You will need to decide whether to provide the vocabulary and structures or to help learners develop strategies for finding this information on their own.

Learners may be directed to make use of corpora to find out which words are commonly used together. Search engines also may be used effectively. Direct learners to put a phrase about which they are unsure (often one translated directly from the L1 to the L2) in quotation marks and to perform an internet search. This approach will help learners to see whether their hypothesized method of expressing an idea is used in the target language.

Responsibilities of Speakers

Speaker responsibilities fall into three categories:[12]

1. *Construction* refers to the debater's obligation to bring new substantive matter to the round; in other words, each debater should develop arguments to support his or her team's position.
2. *Deconstruction* has to do with the obligation to address the constructive matter advanced by teams on the other side of the debate. Debaters should discuss the weaknesses and shortcomings in their opponents' arguments.
3. *Framing* refers to the duty to place the debater's constructive and deconstructive efforts into context. Speakers should point out how their arguments are relevant to the question posed by the motion.

In a typical debate, the first speaker on the proposition will introduce the issue and explain how the argument should be perceived. In addition, the speaker should offer examples that support the proposition's position.

Accordingly, the first order of business for the opposition is to refute the claims just presented by the proposition (deconstruction) and offer a counterargument coupled with evidence that supports their respective position (construction). This type of back and forth continues through the final speakers, who present the closing arguments for their sides. Their remarks should tie together previous speakers' remarks, both deconstructive and constructive, rather than introduce new material. As such, final speakers should take careful notes throughout the debate in order to recap their position's arguments effectively.

The Debate Process

Language exercises culminate in the form of debates conducted in the target language between fellow class members. Teachers may use a variety of methods to organize debates, ranging from town meetings, to Lincoln–Douglas debates, to Socratic discussions. A wide variety of debate methods are available, only some of which we have detailed here. We begin with the more formalized team debate approaches, which follow strict rules related to timing, size of teams, and format. However, we recommend that teachers find the style of debate that works best for the goals of the course. For a course focused primarily on developing language skills, "looser" formats may be just as effective. In a content-based course in which learners are taught formal debate strategies, teachers may find parliamentary debate, Karl Popper debate, or Lincoln–Douglas debate preferable.

Parliamentary Debate

Team members determine in advance the order of speakers and discuss general strategy in terms of issues to define and points to argue. The proposition begins each debate by framing a motion with the wording, "This House believes . . . " or "This House would . . . ." For example, if the motion was "This House believes that governments should mandate wealth redistribution," then the proposition (or "Government") speakers would explain why wealth redistribution is a good idea, and the opposition would demonstrate why it is not. Additionally, the government would propose a course of action and support it with philosophical, practical, and consequential arguments. The burden of proof is on the government, but the opposition also needs to demonstrate the strength of its arguments.

Individual speeches alternate between the proposition and opposition and last between four to seven minutes, depending on the level of students. After the first minute and before the last minute of a speech, any member of the opposing team can offer an argument or ask a question, otherwise known as offering "points of information." For example, when any member of the proposition team is speaking, any member of the opposition team can stand for a point of information. We recommend the following method for signaling time:

1. Yellow card: At the start of the first and last minute, the instructor/ judge holds up a yellow card to signal to members of the opposing team that they may not offer points of information.
2. Green card: When the first minute is up, the instructor/judge holds up a green card that signals to members of the opposing team that they can offer points of information.
3. Red card: When the final minute has ended, the instructor/judge holds up a red card that signals to the speaker that he or she must stop and sit down.

Students are allowed to reference notes for talking points, but they are not allowed to read from them, thus underscoring the extemporaneous aspect of public speaking and the need to think on their feet.

Additionally, synchronous videoconference debates provide an excellent opportunity for participants to interact with native speakers of the foreign language and test their presentational speech abilities. Arrange a series of debates with another instructor. You may choose to find an instructor in the country where your language is spoken natively, in which case the language of the debate will alter from one debate to the next. For instance, the first debate will be in German and the next debate in English. Select topics ahead of time and assign positions. When possible, assign positions that appear counter to the culturally held values of each side. This approach can encourage critical thinking because it forces individuals to try to understand other perspectives than their own.

When synchronous video debates are not possible, consider hosting asynchronous online debates, in which one or two students record an argument, post it on the Web, and then get a response later, ideally from native speakers of the target language. This approach may alleviate difficulties with scheduling.

Karl Popper Debates

In this style of debate, two teams of three argue against each other, one known as the affirmative team, which argues for the proposition, and the other known as the negative team. Rather than "points of information," the focus of the Karl Popper debate is on cross-examination. Participants are assigned numbers, A1, A2, or A3 for the affirmative team and N1, N2, or N3 for members of the negative team. The numbers are important for the order of the arguments and cross-examinations. If the rules of this form of debate are strictly followed, it takes forty-four minutes to complete the procedure, the steps of which are outlined below.

1. Affirmative construction (six minutes). Team member A1 offers the team's complete argument in favor of the resolution.
2. Negative cross-examination (three minutes). N3 questions A1 about the content of his or her argument. Both participants face the audience rather than each other and are not allowed to give speeches; at this point N3 may only ask questions and A1 may only respond to the queries.
3. Negative construction (six minutes). Team member N1 offers his or her team's complete argument against the resolution. It is at this point that the negative team can challenge any definitions set forth by their opponents; if the definitions are not challenged, they are considered to stand.
4. Affirmative cross-examination (three minutes). A3 poses questions to N1, as in the negative cross-examination.
5. Affirmative rebuttal (five minutes). Team member A2 has two primary tasks in this rebuttal. The first is to outline the team's refutations of the opposing team's arguments. Second, he or she must respond to the counterarguments made by the negative team.
6. Negative cross-examination (three minutes). This cross-examination proceeds in the same manner as previous cross-examinations. N1 is responsible for questioning A2.
7. Negative rebuttal (five minutes). As in the affirmative rebuttal, N2 must both refute the opposing team's primary arguments and respond to the refutations made by the affirmative team.
8. Affirmative cross-examination (three minutes). In this cross-examination, A1 asks the questions while N2 responds.

9. Affirmative rebuttal (5 minutes). In this final rebuttal, A3 must be reactive. He or she should renew refutations that have been inadequately addressed by pointing out flaws in the negative rebuttal. He or she may also present additional evidence for existing arguments and try to rest the case of the affirmative team.
10. Negative rebuttal (five minutes). In essence, this rebuttal, offered by N3, follows the procedures outlined for the affirmative team's final rebuttal.

The advantage of this form of debate for an advanced-level language class is that it allows both monologues and dialogues—in the form of the cross-examinations. Teachers need not follow the rules entirely and may not hold their students to the same standards as judged debates.

Lincoln–Douglas Debates

The rules of Lincoln–Douglas debates are similar to the Karl Popper debate rules, with each team member playing a set role at various stages of the debate. Differences reside primarily in the length of time afforded to each portion of the debate, and the fact that the affirmative team both begins and ends the debate. The basic format is as follows:

1. Affirmative constructive (six minutes)
2. Cross-examination of affirmative team by negative team (three minutes)
3. Negative constructive (seven minutes)
4. Cross-examination of negative team by affirmative team (three minutes)
5. Affirmative rebuttal (four minutes)
6. Negative rebuttal and summary (six minutes)
7. Affirmative rebuttal and summary (three minutes)

Alternative Debate Formats

While parliamentary, Karl Popper, and Lincoln–Douglas debates follow very strict rules in debate competitions, teachers can choose the formats that best suit their classes or with which they are more comfortable. Possible variations of individual or team debates are listed below. Some of the formats may be best used before a debate to help learners begin to grapple with the issues, or perhaps even following a debate, after audience members have watched two teams debate an issue.

Presidential Debate

In this format, debates are not team events but individual efforts. Students go head to head with one opponent. The format of presidential debates varies from event to event, but usually a moderator addresses a question to one of the debaters, who is given a certain amount of time (usually two minutes) to respond. His or her opponent is then given one minute to respond. Candidates take turns being the first or second responder. Instruct students not directly participating to closely observe their classmates and to make a list of the points made by each team and the counterarguments to each one.

Tag-Team Debate

This strategy can be used prior to a debate to help students learn about a topic, but it can also be used as a post-debate discussion or instead of one of the team debate methods. In a tag-team debate, each team of five members is awarded a set amount of time (perhaps five minutes) to present its point of view. When it is time for the team to speak, one member takes the floor. He or she is allowed to speak for no more than sixty seconds before "tagging" a member of the team to pick up the argument. Team members may signal to the speaker that they would like to be tagged, but no team member may speak a second time until all members of the team have spoken once.

Town Meetings

One approach to facilitating expression of opinions and argumentation is a mock town meeting in which individual students are assigned particular roles. One advantage of this approach is that it can be less threatening for students to play a role than to express their own opinions on a particular topic. Town meeting–style discussions also allow for a variety of perspectives rather than the either/or approach of a two-sided debate.

Forced Debates

All students who agree with a proposition sit on one side of the room, while all who disagree sit on the opposite side. Form three- or four-member teams among students on the same side of the room, and pair them with a team from the opposite side. Unexpectedly force learners to argue a position counter to their own.

Timed Pair Share

Pair up students who hold different views on a given issue. One student shares his or her ideas for a specified amount of time while the other partner takes notes. Partners reverse roles and follow the same procedure for the specified time. At the conclusion, partners report back on the main issues discussed. Teachers may choose to have one student share his or her partner's ideas with the class.

Paraphrase Passport

This is similar to the timed pair share approach but may utilize teams of three or four students rather than pairs. In addition, before teammates can contribute any ideas of their own, they must paraphrase or restate the ideas of the team member who has just spoken.

Affirmation Passport

This approach is similar to the paraphrase passport except that team members are expected to make a positive statement about comments made by classmates. For example, they may praise the comment's creativity, clarity, or most persuasive point. Once team members have affirmed a comment, they can add their own.

Response Gambits

As in the earlier exercises, before contributing their own comments, team members must first provide a response to other members' statements before providing their own. To facilitate responses to their teammates, students can be given response stems or sentence starters such as, "One thing I learned from your contribution was . . . ," or "Tell me more about . . . ," or "I agree with your point about . . . ."

Talking Chips

To ensure that all members of a team are contributing, distribute a symbolic "talking chip" (e.g., bingo chips, checkers, cards) to each member of three- or four-member teams. As each team member makes a contribution to the discussion, he or she puts the talking chip in the center of the table. Teammates can speak in any order, but they cannot speak a second time until all of the chips are in the center of the table—an indication that everyone has made a contribution. After all of the chips have been placed in the center of the table, team members retrieve their respective chips and begin a second round of discussion.

Response Mode Chips

This is similar in procedure to the talking chips activity except that team members are given several differently labeled or colored chips to represent different types of responses to their teammates (e.g., a "continue brainstorming" chip, a "summarizing" chip, or an "evaluation" chip). They must use one of the response modes during the first round of discussion, relinquishing the corresponding chip after using a particular response type and waiting until all participants have used one of their chips before participating again. In subsequent rounds, participants use their remaining response mode chips. Students may choose the order in which to use their response chips, or the instructor may direct them to use response chips in a particular order if he or she wishes to focus on particular conversational gambits.

Socratic Discussion

Another technique that can be used to generate discussion at a high level is the Socratic discussion or dialogue. Unlike debates, in which individual speakers try to win the argument by listening to their opponents primarily to find weaknesses and offer counterarguments, a dialogue allows shared understanding. The benefits of Socratic discussions are many: they allow students to work together, listen to and respond to one another, and change points of view, as appropriate. Dialogues also allow learners to practice getting and holding the floor as well as techniques for drawing others into the discussion.

Socratic discussions should be set up in a semicircle so that all members of the group can see each other and interact directly, without the intervention of the teacher. In some cases, the teacher may wish to set up an inner circle and an outer circle. Students in the inner circle participate in the discussion while students in the outer circle observe, take notes, and provide feedback.

In addition to grading learners on features of their speech, participants in Socratic discussions may be graded on their ability to take the floor politely, the extent to which they use active listening skills, and their facility with drawing others into the conversation.

Assessing Performance

Criteria for assessing a debate performance fall under two general categories: matter and manner.[13]

Matter

Matter is *what* you say. It is the substance of your speech. As such, matter can be divided into arguments and examples. An *argument* is a statement in which the argument fills in for the X (e.g., "The topic is true [or false, depending on which side you are on] because of X"). If we were debating the topic of higher education versus field experience, an argument might be: "Field experience is more useful than higher education because it allows one to put theory into practice." An *example* is a fact or piece of evidence that supports an argument. If our argument is that field experience is more useful than higher education because it allows one to put theory into practice, then an example might be as follows: "Mark Zuckerberg, the founder of Facebook, and Bill Gates, the founder of Microsoft, both dropped out of Harvard." Only examples relevant to the topic at hand should be used. Examples that have very little or nothing to do with the topic weaken a speech and show a lack of substance.

Matter must be more than just a long list of examples. Facts are like bricks in a wall: If you do not use them and cement them together properly, then they are useless. Similarly, solely disproving some of the facts of the opposition does not necessarily win a debate. Doing so may weaken their case in the same way that removing some bricks from a wall weakens the overall structure, but you really need to attack the main arguments that the other side presents in order to bring the whole wall crashing down.

Manner

Manner is *how* one presents an argument, and there is no prescribed way to go about doing this. As such, speakers should develop a manner style that is natural to them. The following are some tips and pointers on how a speaker can develop an individual style.

1. *Cue cards.* Cue cards should be used in the same way as prompts in a play, i.e., they serve as a reference. Speeches should not be written down on cue cards. Debating represents an exercise in lively interaction between two teams and between the teams and the audience, not in reading a speech.
2. *Eye contact.* Looking at the audience holds their attention. Conversely, reading from cue cards or looking at a point just above the audience loses their attention.
3. *Voice.* While projecting one's voice is important, four minutes of constant shouting becomes annoying very quickly. Adjusting volume, pitch, and speed all help to emphasize important points in a speech. A sudden loud burst will grab the audience's attention; a period of quiet speaking can draw the audience in and make them listen carefully.
4. *Body.* Making hand gestures, moving one's head and upper body to maintain eye contact with members of the audience, pacing back and forth, or even standing still—all of these motions should be done deliberately and with confidence. Body movements should not apologize for the speaker's presence by appearing nervous.
5. *Nervous habits.* Playing with cue cards, pulling on a stray strand of hair, fiddling with a watch, bouncing up and down on the balls of the feet, and so on are nervous habits that detract from a speaker's presentation and should be avoided.
6. *Elocution.* Speakers should try to avoid being too informal without also going overboard the other way. There are no marks to be gained from using big words that one neither understands nor can pronounce.

Speaker Points

These are frequently awarded according to the system depicted in appendix C. Additionally, we recommend using a rubric that reflects a synthesis of criteria developed by ACTFL (see appendix B, "Rubric for Writing and Speaking"). This rubric can be used in conjunction with the system of awarding speaker points depicted in appendix C or independent of it. If superimposed on each other, the category of "Content" in the ACTFL rubric clearly lines up with "Matter," whereas the categories of "Vocabulary," "Grammar," "Structure," and "Impact" correlate with "Manner."

Suggested Speaking Assignment

As the saying goes, "Repetition is the mother of learning," and such wisdom certainly applies to the skill of speaking. Recorded monologues particularly suit the format of a debate course and consist of students video recording themselves giving a five-minute persuasive speech based on the topic under consideration. Students submit their recordings electronically and receive written feedback the following week from the instructor or native speaker assistant. To increase learner motivation, teachers may consider asking learners to record podcasts that other classmates can subscribe to and comment on. This way they receive feedback relevant not only to language skills but also to the content of their recordings. Learners also may watch native speakers discussing the same issue to compare their own performance against that of more competent speakers.

In terms of assessing students' speeches, we recommend referring to the aforementioned systems for awarding speaker points (see appendices B and C). Time permitting during class periods, show students one or two sample student recordings and invite constructive feedback from members of the class.

Self-Assessment and Self-Reflection

After debating a topic, learners should be given an opportunity to self-assess and reflect on their overall performance. For example, ask students to think back over the work that they have done in relation to a debate topic and respond to the following statements choosing one of six possible descriptors (completely disagree, somewhat disagree, disagree, somewhat agree, agree, or completely agree): (1) I felt prepared to debate this topic; (2) I was motivated to debate this topic; and (3) I put a lot of effort into preparing to debate this topic. If students report that they tended to disagree with the statements, ask them what they could do in order to be able to agree with them. If they report that they already agree with the statements, ask them what they could do in order to continue to agree with them. Finally, ask students to identify ten key vocabulary words that they learned and used relative to a topic and that they feel will be most beneficial to them when debating.

Proper self-assessment can heighten students' awareness of skills that they can and cannot carry out effectively and help them in setting learning goals. To enhance the accuracy of student assessments, we recommend setting aside time during class at the beginning of the course to train students in using a rubric designed for such a purpose. Training students to assess their own work and that of others likewise fosters a sense of self-reliance as students learn to evaluate rather than rely on others to point out their strengths and weaknesses. This approach also encourages participants to learn *how* to learn, equipping them with skills that extend beyond the classroom (Jourdenais and Shaw 2005). In addition to assessing their own work, learners may also benefit from sharing strategies that they employed throughout the debate process, along with challenges encountered and solutions discovered (Weissberg 2006). Self-reflection activities can serve as a valuable way to generate intense and thought-provoking discussions while also providing a chance to bring closure to one topic and transition to the next topic.

Conclusion

Finding a Good Fit

When considering whether to implement such a methodology, carefully consider your audience. For example, with regard to oral proficiency, findings from pre- and post-OPI testing suggest that students at the Advanced level and higher benefit more from a debate-oriented approach than those at lower levels; however, findings with regard to written proficiency suggest that one's beginning proficiency level factors less in determining gain than scaffolded learning in the form of methodical revisions to writing assignments.[14]

Candid Input from Instructors and Students

Instructor and student input has played an integral role in the development of this pedagogical approach. In addition to soliciting student evaluations at the conclusion of each course, we routinely presented findings at national and international conferences and received invaluable feedback and suggestions from colleagues. The methodology also benefited from thoughtful external reviews of articles that we submitted for publication to journals in the field of second language acquisition.

Such a curriculum demands much of both instructors and students. Some instructors have expressed that they feel inadequate to the task but have compensated by team teaching with a native speaker assistant. Likewise, students can feel overwhelmed at first, especially if too much is expected of them in too short a time. As such, we urge instructors to tailor the pace and sophistication of the course to the general proficiency level of the learners in order to maximize the benefits of scaffolded exercises and to promote sustained growth.

On the whole, the feedback has been very encouraging, and we hope that both instructors and students will benefit greatly from this brief overview of teaching foreign languages through global debate.

Appendices

Appendix A: Sample Graphic Organizers

1. Cause-Effect. Add more boxes as needed.

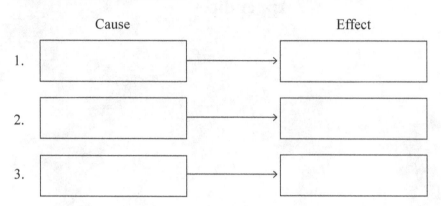

2. Problem-Solution. Add more boxes as needed.

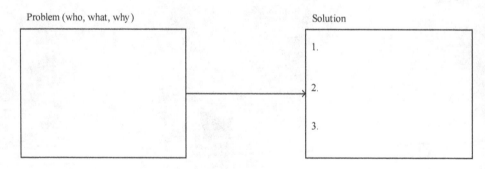

3. Argument. Add more boxes as needed.

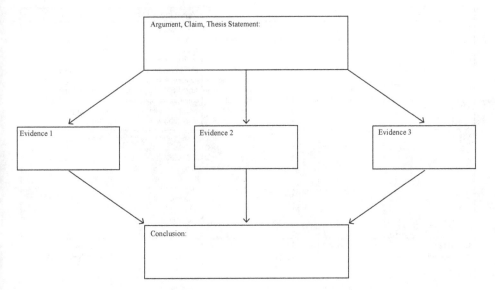

4. For/Against

Position	For	Against

Appendix B: Rubric for Writing and Speaking

Criteria	Fair	Good	Very Good	Excellent
Content Appropriate and complete content, including introduction and conclusion	**10-13 points** Writer/speaker fails to support his/her claim for various reasons, which may include lack of evidence or analysis for arguments, inability to respond to opposing arguments.	**14-15 points** Writer/speaker somewhat successfully supports his/her claim. Some evidence or analysis is offered for arguments. Is somewhat able to reply to opposing argument.	**16-17 points** Writer/speaker successfully supports his/her claim. He/she is able to establish a clear position with adequate support. Writer/speaker counters the opposing side's arguments reasonably well.	**18-20 points** Writer/speaker makes powerful arguments in support of his/her claim, uses inconsistencies in opposing arguments to his/her advantage, and shows awareness of the complexity of the issue.
Vocabulary Accuracy, variety, and appropriateness of word choice	**10-13 points** Vocabulary demonstrates inadequate range and/or inaccuracy. Meaning is confused.	**14-15 points** Limited range of vocabulary; use of words is sometimes inaccurate or inappropriate.	**16-17 points** Vocabulary is adequate and includes some idiomatic expressions, though writer/speaker may use general terminology rather than specific. Use of words is occasionally inaccurate.	**18-20 points** Vocabulary is sophisticated in range and sociolinguistically appropriate.
Grammar Accuracy, form	**10-13 points** Major problems in simple and complex constructions; frequent errors of agreement, tense, number, case, etc.	**14-15 points** Effective but simple constructions, minor problems in complex constructions, several errors of agreement, tense, number, and case.	**16-17 points** Effective complex constructions, few errors of agreement, tense, number, or case.	**18-20 points** Virtually no errors.
Structure Quantity and organization of language discourse	**10-13 points** Variety of complete sentences and cohesive devices. In writing, emerging paragraph-length discourse. Inadequate introduction and/or conclusion.	**14-15 points** Thoughts are logically presented. In writing, complete paragraphs, with clear structure and cohesive devices; adequate introduction and conclusion.	**16-17 points** Language moves beyond individual thoughts to a connected whole. In writing, paragraphs are logically structured with adequate introduction and conclusion.	**18-20 points** Discourse is well organized and structured around a single theme. In writing, effective introduction and conclusion frame logically structured paragraphs in the main body.
Impact Ability to motivate the audience to continue reading or listening	**10-13 points** Writing or speech lacks fluency; speech is filled with lengthy pauses; writing is disjointed. The audience would quickly become impatient with this essay/speech.	**14-15 points** Writing or speech is somewhat choppy. The audience would find the essay/speech difficult to follow.	**16-17 points** Writing or speech is smooth and fluid. The audience would find this essay/speech engaging to read or listen to.	**18-20 points** Writing or speech is fluent, with a definite style. The audience would be very motivated to read/listen to this essay/speech.
Name:_____		Total Points (100 points possible) _____		

Note: To download a PDF of the illustrations in this book, please visit http://press.georgetown.edu/book/languages/teaching-advanced-language-skills-through-global-debate.

Appendix C: Speaker Points Scoring Guide

Matter	Manner	Total	Meaning
50.0	50.0	100	Flawless
47.5	47.5	95	Excellent
45.0	45.0	90	Very Good
42.5	42.5	85	Good
40.0	40.0	80	Above Average
37.5	37.5	75	Average
35.0	35.0	70	Below Average
32.5	32.5	65	Poor
30.0	30.0	60	Very Poor
27.5	27.5	55	Bad
25.0	25.0	50	Very Bad

Note: To download a PDF of the illustrations in this book, please visit http://press.georgetown.edu/book/languages/teaching-advanced-language-skills-through-global-debate.

Notes

1. For the Russian volume, see Brown et al. 2014. For the English volume, see Talalakina et al. 2014.

2. We wish to thank Cynthia Martin of the University of Maryland for providing invaluable input with regard to ACTFL proficiency guidelines.

3. See www.actfl.org for studies on the reliability and validity of the OPI as an assessment instrument and for more information about tester training and certification.

4. There have been three editions of the guidelines: 1986, 1999, and 2012. In all versions, the major levels have remained the same, with a Distinguished level added to the 2012 edition.

5. Although the 2012 guidelines added a Distinguished level, the current official OPI does not test for Distinguished. A brief discussion of the Distinguished level and considerations for assessment can be found at the end of this introduction.

6. ACTFL, *Can-Do Statements: Progress Indicators for Language Learners*, accessed February 14, 2014, http://www.actfl.org/sites/default/files/pdfs/Can-Do_Statements.pdf, p. 5.

7. Council of Europe, *Common European Framework of Reference for Languages: Learning, Teaching, Assessment*, accessed February 14, 2014, http://www.coe.int/t/dg4/linguistic/Source/Framework_EN.pdf, p. 6.

8. Ibid.

9. Over fifteen centuries ago, the Chinese historian Kuan Ch'en described competitive debates referred to as "Pure Talk."

10. For a detailed comparison of the British and American debate systems, refer to Wallace (1992).

11. While pronunciation may impact listeners' initial perception of a speaker's ability to construct a logical and cohesive argument, the well-known "Kissinger effect," or ability to debate skillfully despite clear deficiencies in pronunciation, must be taken into account.

12. Adapted from "The Cabin Fever Debates," University of Alaska Anchorage, accessed March 1, 2014, http://www.uaa.alaska.edu/seawolfdebate/Cabin FeverDebates/.

13. Adapted from "Basic Debating Skills," ACT Debating Union, accessed March 1, 2014, http://www.actdu.org.au/archives/actein_site/basicskills.html.

14. For additional reading regarding these findings, see Brown (2009).

References

Adair-Hauck, Bonnie, Eileen W. Glisan, and Francis J. Troyan. 2013. *Implementing Integrated Performance Assessment*. Alexandria, VA: American Council on the Teaching of Foreign Languages.

American Council on the Teaching of Foreign Languages (ACTFL). 1982. "ACTFL Language Proficiency Projects." *Modern Language Journal* 66, no. 2: 179.

———. 2012. *ACTFL Proficiency Guidelines 2012*. Alexandria, VA: American Council on the Teaching of Foreign Languages. www.actfl.org/sites/default/files/pdfs/public/ACTFLProficiencyGuidelines2012\eFINAL.pdf.

Anderson, Neil J. 2005. "L2 Strategy Research." In *Handbook of Research in Second Language Teaching and Learning*, edited by Eli Hinkel, 757–72. Mahwah, NJ: Erlbaum Associates.

Anderson, Neil J., and ZhaoHong Han. 2009. *Second Language Reading Research and Instruction: Crossing the Boundaries*. Ann Arbor: University of Michigan Press.

Beck, Isabel L., Margaret G. McKeown, Rebecca Hamilton, and Linda Kucan. 1997. *Questioning the Author: An Approach for Enhancing Student Engagement with Text*. Newark, DE: International Reading Association.

Bernhardt, Elizabeth. 2001. "Research into the Teaching of Literature in a Second Language: What It Says and How to Communicate It to Graduate Students." In *SLA and the Literature Classroom: Fostering Dialogues*, edited by Virginia M. Scott and Holly Tucker, 195–210. Boston: Heinle & Heinle.

———. 2005. "Progress and Procrastination in Second Language Reading." *Annual Review of Applied Linguistics* 25:135–50.

Bransford, John D., and Marcia K. Johnson. 1972. "Contextual Prerequisites for Understanding: Some Investigations of Comprehension and Recall." *Journal of Verbal Learning and Verbal Behavior* 11:717–26.

Brecht, Richard D., Dan E. Davidson, and Ralph B. Ginsberg. 1995. "Predictors of Foreign Language Gain During Study Abroad." In *Second Language Acquisition in a Study Abroad Context*, edited by Barbara F. Freed, 37–66. Amsterdam: John Benjamins.

Brown, N. Anthony. 2009. "Argumentation and Debate in Foreign Language Instruction: A Case for the Traditional Classroom Facilitating Advanced Level Language Uptake." *Modern Language Journal* 93, no. 4: 534–49.

Brown, N. Anthony, Jennifer Bown, and Dennis L. Eggett. 2009. "Making Rapid Gains in Second Language Writing: A Case Study of a Third-Year Russian Language Course." *Foreign Language Annals* 42, no. 3: 424–53.

Brown, Tony, Tatiana M. Balykhina, Ekaterina V. Talalakina, Jennifer Bown, and Viktoria B. Kurilenko. 2014. *Mastering Russian through Global Debate*. Washington, DC: Georgetown University Press.

Clarke, Mark A. 1980. "The Short Circuit Hypothesis of ESL Reading: Or When Language Competence Interferes with Reading Performance." *Modern Language Journal* 64:203–9.

Clifford, Ray T., and Troy L. Cox. 2013. "Empirical Validation of Reading Proficiency Guidelines." *Foreign Language Annals* 46:45–61.

Connor, Ulla. 1987. "Argumentative Patterns in Student Essays: Cross-cultural Differences." In *Writing across Languages: Analysis of L2 Text*, edited by Ulla Connor and Robert Kaplan, 57–71. Reading, MA: Addison-Wesley.

Cooper, Thomas C. 1981. "Sentence Combining: An Experiment in Teaching Writing." *Modern Language Journal* 65:158–65.

Coyle, Do, Philip Hood, and David Marsh. 2010. *CLIL: Content and Language Integrated Learning*. Cambridge: Cambridge University Press.

Ferguson, Charles. 1959. "Diglossia." *Word* 15:325–40.

Fessenden, Seth A., Roy I. Johnson, P. Merville Johnson, and Kaye M. Good. 1973. *Speech for the Creative Teacher*. Dubuque, IA: Wm. C. Brown.

Gascoigne, Carolyn. 2002. "Documenting the Initial Second Language Reading Experience: The Readers Speak." *Foreign Language Annals* 35:554–60.

Grabe, William. 2009. *Reading in a Second Language: Moving from Theory to Practice*. New York: Cambridge University Press.

Grabe, William, and Fredericka L. Stoller. 2011. *Teaching and Researching Reading*. London: Longman.

Graves, Michael F., Melanie Ruda, Gregory C. Sales, and James F. Baumann. 2012. "Teaching Prefixes: Making Strong Instruction Even Stronger." In *Vocabulary Instruction: Research to Practice*, edited by Edward J. Kame'enui and James F. Baumann, 95–115. New York: Guilford.

Hedegaard, Mariane. 2005. "The Zone of Proximal Development as Basis for Instruction." In *An Introduction to Vygotsky*, 2nd ed., edited by Harry Daniels, 227–51. London: Routledge.

Higgs, Theodore V., and Ray T. Clifford. 1982. "The Push toward Communication." In *Curriculum Competence and the Foreign Language Teacher*. ACTFL Foreign Language Education Series 13, edited by Theodore V. Higgs, 57–59. Lincolnwood, IL: National Textbook.

Inch, Edward S., and Barbara Warnick. 2005. *Critical Thinking and Communication: The Use of Reason in Argument*, 5th ed. Boston: Allyn and Bacon.

Jensen, Linda. 1986. "Advanced Reading Skills in a Comprehensive Course." In *Teaching Second Language Reading for Academic Purposes*, edited by Fraida Dubin, David Eskey, and William Grabe, 103–24. Reading, MA: Addison-Wesley.

Jourdenais, Richard M., and Peter A. Shaw. 2005. "Dimensions of Content-Based Instruction in Second Language Education." In *Content, Tasks and Projects in the Language Classroom: 2004 Conference Proceedings*, edited by Richard M. Jourdenais and Sarah E. Springer, 1–12. Monterey, CA: Monterey Institute of International Studies.

Kaplan, Robert B. 1987. "Cultural Thought Patterns Revisited." In *Writing across Languages: Analysis of L2 Text*, edited by Ulla Connor and Robert B. Kaplan, 9–21. Reading, MA: Addison-Wesley.

Kennedy, George. 1984. *New Testament Interpretation through Rhetorical Criticism*. Chapel Hill: University of North Carolina Press.

Laufer, Batia. 1997. "The Lexical Plight in Second Language Reading: Words You Don't Know, Words You Think You Know, and Words You Can't Guess." In *Second Language Vocabulary Acquisition*, edited by James Coady and Thomas Huckin, 20–34. New York: Cambridge University Press.

Laufer, Batia, and Gecke C. Ravenhorst-Kalovski. 2010. "Lexical Threshold Revisited: Lexical Text Coverage, Learners' Vocabulary Size and Reading Comprehension." *Reading in a Foreign Language* 22:15–30.

Leaver, Betty L., and Marsha A. Kaplan. 2004. "Task-Based Instruction in US Government Slavic Language Programs." In *Task-Based Instruction in Foreign Language Education: Practice and Programs*, edited by Betty L. Leaver and Jane R. Willis, 47–66. Washington, DC: Georgetown University Press.

Leaver, Betty L., and Boris Shekhtman. 2002. "Principles and Practices in Teaching Superior-level Language Skills: Not Just More of the Same." In *Developing Professional-Level Language Proficiency*, edited by Betty L. Leaver and Boris Shekhtman, 3–33. Cambridge: Cambridge University Press.

Long, Michael H. 2007. *Problems in SLA*. Mahwah, NJ: Erlbaum Associates.

Lund, Randall J. 1990. "A Comparison of Second Language Listening and Reading Comprehension." *Modern Language Journal* 75:196–204.

Magnan, Sally S., and Michele Back. 2007. "Social Interaction and Linguistic Gain during Study Abroad." *Foreign Language Annals* 45:43–61.

Massie, J. 2005. "Consideration of Context in the CBI Course Development Process." In *Content, Tasks and Projects in the Language Classroom: 2004 Conference*

Proceedings, edited by Richard M. Jourdenais and Sarah E. Springer, 79–91. Monterey, CA: Monterey Institute of International Studies.

Maxim, Hiram H., II. 2002. "A Study into the Feasibility and Effects of Reading Extended Authentic Discourse in the Beginning German Language Classroom." *Modern Language Journal* 86:20–35.

Meyer, Bonnie J. F. 1987. "Following the Author's Top-Level Structure: An Important Skill for Reading Comprehension." In *Understanding Readers' Understanding*, edited by Robert J. Tierney, Judy N. Mitchell, and Patricia L. Anders, 59–76. Hillsdale, NJ: Erlbaum Associates.

MLA Ad Hoc Committee on Foreign Languages. 2007. *Foreign Language and Higher Education: New Structures for a Changed World.* New York: The Modern Language Association of America. Accessed March 1, 2014. www.mla.org/pdf/forlang_news_pdf.pdf.

Nation, Paul. 1990. *Teaching and Learning Vocabulary.* New York: Newbury House.

———. 1997. "The Language Learning Benefits of Extensive Reading." *Language Teacher Online*, May 21. http://jalt-publications.org/old_tlt/files/97/may/benefits.html.

———. 2006. "How Large a Vocabulary Is Needed for Reading and Listening?" *Canadian Modern Language Review* 63:59–82.

Palmer, Harold E. 1968. *The Scientific Study and Teaching of Languages.* Oxford: Oxford University Press. Originally published London: Harrap, 1917.

Paribakht, Tahereh S, and Marjorie Wesche. 1996. "Enhancing Vocabulary Acquisition through Reading: A Hierarchy of Text-Related Exercise Types." *Canadian Modern Language Review* 52:250–73.

———. 1997. "Vocabulary Enhancement Activities and Reading for Meaning in Second Language Vocabulary Development." In *Second Language Vocabulary Acquisition*, edited by James Coady and Thomas Huckin, 174–200. New York: Cambridge University Press.

Philipsen, Gerry. 1992. *Speaking Culturally: Explorations in Social Communication.* Albany: State University of New York Press.

Powell, Steve. 2005. "Extensive Reading and Its Role in Japanese High Schools." *Reading Matrix* 5, no. 2: 28–42.

Prabhu, N. S. 1987. *Second Language Pedagogy.* Oxford: Oxford University Press.

Pulido, Diana, and David Z. Hambrick. 2008. "The Virtuous Circle: Modeling Individual Differences and L2 Reading and Vocabulary Development." *Reading in a Foreign Language* 20:164–90.

Redding, W. Charles. 1954. "Composition of the Debate Speech." In *Argumentation and Debate: Principles and Practices*, edited by D. Potter, 193–213. New York: Dryden Press.

Renandya, Willy A., and Thomas S. C. Farrell. 2011. "Teacher, the Tape Is Too Fast: Extensive Listening in ELT." *ELT Journal* 65, no. 1: 52–59.

Rost, Michael. 2011. *Teaching and Researching Listening*. New York: Longman.

Sample, Mark. 2012. "A Better Blogging Assignment." *Humanities and Technology Camp Blog*. June 11, 2012. Accessed September 12, 2014. http://chnm2012 .thatcamp.org/06/11/a-better-blogging-assignment/.

Samuels, S. Jay. 1979. "The Method of Repeated Readings." *Reading Teacher* 32:403–8.

Schmidt, Richard W., and Sylvia Nagem Frota. 1990. "Developing Basic Conversational Ability in a Second Language: A Case Study of an Adult Learner of Portuguese." In *Talking to Learn: Conversation in Second Language Acquisition*, edited by Richard R. Day, 237–326.

Schmitt, Norbert. 2008. "Instructed Second Language Vocabulary Learning." *Language Teaching Research* 12:329–63.

Schultz, Jean Marie. 1994. "Stylistic Reformulation: Theoretical Premises and Practical Applications." *Modern Language Journal* 78:169–78.

Scott, Virginia M. 1992. "Writing from the Start: A Task-Oriented Developmental Writing Program for Foreign Language Students." In *Dimension Language '91*, edited by R. Terry, 1–15. Southern Conference on Language Teaching. Valdosta, GA: Valdosta State University.

Segalowitz, Norm, Cathy Poulsen, and Mel Komoda. 1991. "Lower Level Components of Reading Skill in Higher Level Bilinguals: Implications for Reading Instruction." *AILA Review* 8:5–14.

Shaw, Peter A. 1997. "With One Stone: Models of Instruction and Their Curricular Implications in an Advanced Content-Based Foreign Language Program." In *Content-Based Instruction in Foreign Language Education: Models and Methods*, edited by Stephen B. Stryker and Betty L. Leaver, 261–82. Washington, DC: Georgetown University Press.

Shrum, Judith L., and Eileen W. Glisan. 2010. *Teacher's Handbook: Contextualized Language Instruction*. Boston: Heinle.

Silva, Tony. 1993. "Toward an Understanding of the Distinct Nature of L2 Writing: The ESL Research and Its Implications." *TESOL Quarterly* 27:665–77.

Stevick, Earl W. 1984. "Similarities and Differences between Oral and Written Comprehension: An Imagist View." *Foreign Language Annals* 17:281–83.

Stryker, Stephen B., and Betty L. Leaver. 1997. "Content-Based Instruction: From Theory to Practice." In *Content-Based Instruction in Foreign Language Education: Models and Methods*, edited by Stephen B. Stryker and Betty L. Leaver, 3–28. Washington, DC: Georgetown University Press.

Swaffar, Janet, and Katherine Arens. 2005. *Remapping the Foreign Language Curriculum: An Approach through Multiple Literacies*. New York: Modern Language Association.

Swain, Merrill. 1993. "The Output Hypothesis: Just Speaking and Writing Aren't Enough." *Canadian Modern Language Review/La Revue canadienne des langues vivantes* 50:158–64.

Talalakina, Ekaterina V., Tony Brown, Jennifer Bown, and William G. Eggington. 2014. *Mastering English through Global Debate*. Washington, DC: Georgetown University Press.

Tschirner, Erwin, and L. Kathy Heilenman. 1998. "Reasonable Expectations: Oral Proficiency Goals for Intermediate-Level Students of German." *Modern Language Journal* 82:147–58.

van Lier, Leo. 2005. "The Bellman's Map: Avoiding the 'Perfect and Absolute Blank' in Language Learning." In *Content, Tasks and Projects in the Language Classroom: 2004 Conference Proceedings*, edited by Richard M. Jourdenais and Peter A. Shaw, 13–21. Monterey, CA: Monterey Institute of International Studies.

Wallace, James. 1992. "Debate: A Cross-cultural Perspective." *Parliamentary Debate* 1, no. 1: 2–24.

Weissberg, Robert. 2006. *Connecting Speaking and Writing in Second Language Instruction*. Ann Arbor: University of Michigan Press.

Williams, Jessica. 2005. *Teaching Writing in Second and Foreign Language Classrooms*. Boston: McGraw Hill.

Willis, Dave. 1996. "Accuracy, Fluency and Conformity." In *Challenge and Change in Language Teaching*, edited by Jane Willis and Dave Willis, 44–51. Oxford: Heinemann Macmillan.

Willis, Jane R. 2004. "Perspectives on Task-Based Instruction: Understanding Our Practices, Acknowledging Different Practitioners." In *Task-Based Instruction in Foreign Language Education: Practice and Programs*, edited by Betty L. Leaver and Jane R. Willis, 3–46. Washington, DC: Georgetown University Press.

Zhu, Yunxia. 2005. *Written Communication across Cultures*. Philadelphia: John Benjamins.

About the Authors

Tony Brown is an associate professor in the department of German and Russian at Brigham Young University. He has published articles in such journals as *Foreign Language Annals, Modern Language Journal, Russian Language Journal*, and *Language Policy*.

Jennifer Bown is an associate professor in the department of German and Russian at Brigham Young University. Her articles have appeared in such journals as *Language Teaching, Foreign Language Annals, Modern Language Journal*, and *Innovation in Language Teaching and Learning*.